DANIEL 1-6

INDUCTIVE BIBLE STUDIES
DISCOVER 4 YOURSELF
FOR KIDS!

YOU'RE A BRAVE MAN, DANIEL!

KAY ARTHUR
JANNA ARNDT

TEACHER GUIDE
Elizabeth A. McAllister, Ed. D.

YOU'RE A BRAVE MAN, DANIEL! TEACHER GUIDE
Published by Precept Ministries of Reach Out, Inc.
P. O. Box 182218
Chattanooga, TN 37422

ISBN 978-1-888655-47-6

D4Y Teacher Guides were made possible by the generous gift of a long-time friend of Precept Ministries.

Author Photo and Cover by John Phillips

Graphics Design by Michele Walker

YOU'RE A BRAVE MAN, DANIEL!

TEACHER GUIDE
TABLE OF CONTENTS

YOU'RE A BRAVE MAN, DANIEL!
TEACHER GUIDE

Introduction

Thank you for selecting this Bible study for your child and/or class. Leading children to read, observe, interpret, and apply the Bible for themselves offers them a bridge from hearsay to real truth. As they learn to be comfortable with the idea that they can read the Bible, they will take the task seriously.

The Discover 4 Yourself series is designed to lead young students through the process of inductive study: question, question, question, search, think, understand, and apply. They will be comfortable with this process only after you prove that the possibility is within their reach.

YOU'RE A BRAVE MAN, DANIEL! is a study of Daniel 1-6. Students will begin with an overview of these chapters to track Daniel's life and discover God's gracious protection through many difficult and frightening tests of character, integrity, and endurance. Daniel and thousands of other Jews were deported from Israel and forced to serve several evil kings in Babylon. You will discover, once again, how God uses every event in your life to further His wonderful purposes and bless you with His presence and salvation.

To prepare for leading **YOU'RE A BRAVE MAN, DANIEL!** please work through each "Day" on your own before consulting the Teacher Guide. Since this is an Inductive Bible Study, your teaching will be more effective if you do the work first and God reveals His truth *to you*.

Whether you're homeschooling a child, teaching a Sunday school class, teaching in a Christian school, or simply using these studies for your child's quiet time or family Bible study, this Teacher Guide will show you how to clearly and carefully lead each child through Inductive Bible study. We offer suggestions to guide you step-by-step. *Instructional Strategies* explains why certain activities are used throughout the book. Choose the activities that best fit your situation.

Homeschooling Parents and Family Bible Study

We suggest you do one "Day" per day unless it's too much for your child's reading and/or writing skills. You can work with your child and discuss what you learn together or let him/her work independently, saving discussion times for later.

You may want to join or create a homeschool group that meets once a week to do these studies. The teacher will assign a week of homework in class. The following week the teacher will lead the students to discuss what they discovered, how to apply it, and to work on any creative elements included in the study or play a game to review what they have learned.

Sunday School Teachers

To use these studies in a weekly Sunday school class we suggest you do one "Day" together with your children each week in class, since you will have children from different backgrounds, even some from families that are not members of or even regularly attend a church.

Each Sunday briefly review the prior Sunday's work to put them in context for the next day of study in their book. After completing a week in the book you may want to have a "Game Time Sunday" to review the material before you move on to the next week. Game time makes learning fun for children and shows you the extent to which they understand what they learned.

You can keep the books at church and have the children take home verses on index cards or pieces of paper to memorize.

Classroom Teachers

Generally, classroom teachers face many different learning abilities within their groups. It is important for you to understand these different learning abilities so that you can meet each child where he or she is so that no one is left behind during the process.

It is important for you to bring in *schemata* (background information) for students to draw on. If you tie studies to something children already know, they will grasp the lessons clearly.

Grasp is also affected by *metacognition*—the ability to monitor understanding of the text. Students must be able to perform several functions to develop metacognitive control over reading and understanding. He or she must be able to:

1. Ask first, "What do I already know about this topic?" then, "Do I have enough information to understand this text?" Answers to these questions will directly influence the use of the inductive method.

2. Identify the purpose for reading each selection.

3. Focus on particular information.

4. Monitor understanding by recalling background knowledge and relating it to the context by asking questions like: "How am I doing?" "Am I keeping the big picture in mind?" "Am I bogged down?" "If so, how do I fix it—reread the passages or ask for help?" (Nothing wrong with the latter.)

5. Evaluate understanding of the context by asking, "What did I learn?" With respect to Inductive Bible Study, "How do I apply this information?"

Instructional Strategies

Writing as a response reinforces learning and so this method is prevalent in these books. Encourage students to share ideas and insights with you and other students.

Reading is the highest intellectual activity of the human experience. More sectors of the brain are active than in other endeavors including mathematics and flying an airplane. It's the most totally interactive processing of information, even when children are reading Mother Goose.

Take time for students to read aloud with a friend. Reading *out loud* and listening promote interactions between the brain's left and right hemispheres and activate little-used pathways. Reading *silently* activates a much smaller part of the brain.

Give students a chance to express themselves at every opportunity. This forces them to retrieve information stored in their *schemata* (background knowledge) for application to new information. What better opportunity is there than to *inductively* look at curriculum and context?

You will notice that you are asked to read some content aloud as students follow along. This frees unsure readers to focus on context rather than decoding strategies. By doing this, you will remove stumbling blocks to understanding; otherwise, reluctant readers will be convinced that inductive study is impossible for them—the last thought you want to instill!

We have included weekly quizzes with memory verses and also multiple-choice questions that will force students to think about what they have learned. Based on how they answer these questions, you will know whether they have grasped the material adequately.

In view of this sparse introduction to learning requirements for success, it's important that you apply strategies that lead students to develop the ability to self-monitor understanding of context each step of the way. These **Teacher Guides** offer suggestions to assure that students, regardless of their abilities, will learn to read the Bible with understanding as you lead them, step-by-step, through the Inductive Study Method.

Discover 4 Yourself Objectives

The Discover 4 Yourself series objectives are not the same as the behavioral objectives of general subject matter. The books contain outstanding biblical subjects of course, but they are written *primarily* to be a tool for young students to learn the Inductive Bible Study Method.

Playing an instrument well requires repetition and application of skills learned. Similarly, effective study is developed by repeated practice and good role modeling of an outstanding study method. Accordingly these **Teacher Guides** contain global objectives for the student *and the teacher*.

We'll start with the teacher.

Discover 4 Yourself Teacher Guide Objectives

✓   To help the teacher identify students' metacognitive needs as they read texts.

✓   To show the teacher how to model use of the Inductive Study Method so students will be able to apply the techniques independently when studying God's Word.

✓   To offer the teacher effective teaching strategies to assure that students succeed when they study the Bible.

Discover 4 Yourself Student Workbook Objectives

✓   To learn how to read, observe, and interpret the Bible for themselves.

✓   To practice this method independently within an encouraging environment.

Scripture quotations in this book are taken from the New American Standard Bible ®, © 1960, 1962, 1963, 1968, 1971, 1972, 1973, 1975, 1977, 1995 by The Lockman Foundation. Used by permission. (*www.Lockman.org*)

DISCOVER 4 YOURSELF is a registered trademark of The Hawkins Children's LLC. Harvest House Publishers, Inc., is the exclusive licensee of the federally registered trademark DISCOVER 4 YOURSELF.

Illustrations © Steve Bjorkman

Cover by Left Coast Design, Portland, Oregon

YOU'RE A BRAVE MAN, DANIEL!

Copyright © 2007 by Precept Ministries International
Published by Harvest House Publishers
Eugene, Oregon 97402
www.harvesthousepublishers.com

ISBN-13: 978-0-7369-0147-5
ISBN-10: 0-7369-0147-7

Printed in the United States of America

07 08 09 10 11 12 13 14 15 / ML-SK / 10 9 8 7 6 5 4 3 2 1

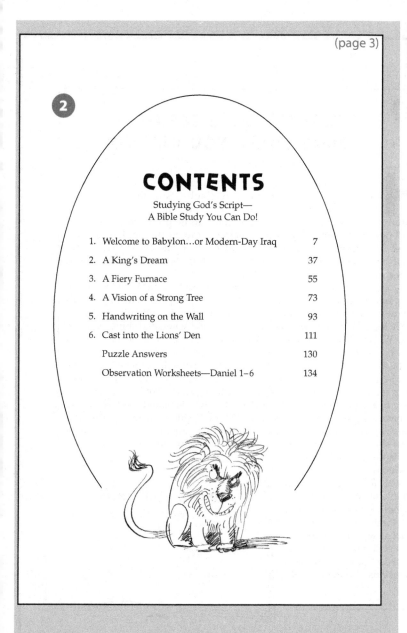

(page 3)

②

CONTENTS

Studying God's Script—
A Bible Study You Can Do!

Guided Instruction

① Give each student a copy of *You're A Brave Man, Daniel!*

② Together, turn to the CONTENTS page and lead students through a quick overview of the book. Point out the structure of each chapter, noting that there will be a lesson and activities to do each day for five days.

"Welcome to Babylon…or Modern-Day Iraq" 7

Max, Molly, and Sam are going to dig into God's Word to discover how a young boy who was kidnapped and made to serve a wicked king handled difficult situations. Daniel loved God and trusted Him. What would you do if your life was turned upside-down and you found yourself in a strange land? This is an exciting story with some surprising events.

"A King's Dream" 37

Wicked King Nebuchadnezzar besieged Jerusalem and took the sons of Israel captive. They were transported to Babylon, an ancient city located in territory occupied by present-day Iraq. Daniel was just fifteen years old. Imagine how you'd feel if you were kidnapped and removed from every familiar place and person in your life. Daniel and his friends were outstanding teenagers who remained true to their God.

"A Fiery Furnace" 55

King Nebuchadnezzar built an image of gold and demanded that everyone bow down and worship it. Daniel's friends, Shadrach, Meshach and Abed-nego, refused. This angered the king and he sentenced them to be burned in a fiery furnace. But Someone came to their rescue!

"A Vision of a Strong Tree" 73

King Nebuchadnezzar called Daniel in to interpret a frightening dream. Daniel told the king that the tree that was chopped down was him. This meant he would become like an animal and live among animals until he acknowledged and worshipped the True God. This should get his attention!

"Handwriting on the Wall" 93

King Nebuchadnezzar died in 562 BC. In 539 BC, King Belshazzar was a wicked king who did not worship the Holy God. He ordered the vessels of the temple of God in Jerusalem to be brought to him for a feast. Then he, his nobles, his wives, and his concubines all drank from them. Suddenly a huge hand began writing on the wall. Scary! He called for Daniel to interpret the writing. That same night he was killed. Was this because he did not glorify God?

"Cast into the Lions' Den" 111

Darius was now king. He appointed Daniel to be one of the commissioners over his kingdom. The other commissioners were jealous of Daniel and decided to find a way to get rid of him. They asked the king to sign a law to force everyone to petition only him. But Daniel continued to pray to his God. When King Darius was told this, he commanded Daniel to be thrown into a lion's den. WHO do you think came to Daniel's rescue? Isn't this an exciting mystery?

③ After leading students through an overview of the Contents, turn to "Studying God's Script—A Bible Study You Can Do!" on page 5.

Guided Instruction

(page 5)

③ STUDYING GOD'S SCRIPT— A BIBLE STUDY YOU CAN DO!

Hey, guys! It's great to have you back on another great Bible adventure. We are on our way (Molly, Sam the great detective beagle, and me) to meet my Aunt Sherry in Hollywood, California. My name is Max. We are going to help out on the set of a brand-new television series that is being made on the Book of Daniel. Daniel is a very interesting, historical book in the Bible that shows us not only WHAT happened in the past, but also WHAT is going to happen in the future. Doesn't that sound *exciting?*

We are going to use God's script, the Bible, to find out WHO the main characters are in the Book of Daniel and WHAT happens to them as God's story unfolds. HOW do Daniel and his friends handle difficult situations? WHAT lessons can we learn about trusting God when bad things happen to us? WHO has visions and dreams? WHAT do these dreams mean? And WHO is in control of all Daniel's circumstances?

This is going to be one *awesome* television series with some unbelievable special effects to capture these special dreams and events! You can take part in creating this exciting series by studying God's Word, the Bible, the source of all truth, and by asking God's Spirit to lead and guide you. You also have this book, which is an inductive Bible study. That word *inductive* means you go straight to the Bible *yourself* to investigate what the Book of Daniel shows us about God and His plan for the future and a young man who is serious about God. In inductive Bible study you discover for yourself what the Bible says and means.

Doesn't that sound like fun? Grab your script on Daniel as we take a look into the past so we can film this action-packed adventure that will take us into the future!

THINGS YOU'LL NEED

New American Standard Bible (Updated Edition)— preferably the New Inductive Study Bible (NISB)

Pen or Pencil   A Dictionary

Colored Pencils   This Workbook

Index Cards

1

WELCOME TO BABYLON… OR MODERN-DAY IRAQ

4

DANIEL 1

It's great to have you here in sunny California! Molly and I are soooo excited about this new Bible adventure where we'll get to help on a brand-new television series. Miss Leslie, the producer of this series, is a friend of my Aunt Sherry, who developed the comic book on the life of Joseph called *Joseph— God's Superhero.*

Miss Leslie asked Aunt Sherry to come out to California to help her create and direct this fantastic television series on the life of Daniel. Aren't you excited? Not only do we get to learn all about Daniel and how to be like him, but we also get to learn how to create and shoot a television series. Are you ready to get started? Great! Then let's head over to the set and start reading God's script.

SCAN THE SCRIPT!

"Hey, guys, I see you made it!" Aunt Sherry said with a smile as we walked on the set. "Are you ready to start studying God's script, the Bible?"

7

Guided Instruction

WEEK 1

DAY ONE

You are about to read a story about God's mercy and compassion. Ask God to give you clear understanding of His awesome love.

4 Turn to page 7 and read the introduction "Daniel 1" and "Scan the Script!"

Guided Instruction

"We sure are!" Max replied as he gave Aunt Sherry a hug.

"Great. Then grab your scripts and have a seat in those chairs."

"Look, Max," Molly exclaimed, "our chairs have our names on the back just like in the movies."

"That is so cool!" Max said with a smile. "Look, Sam! Aunt Sherry even has a chair just for you." Sam jumped up into his chair and sat on his haunches looking like Mr. Hollywood. Aunt Sherry, Max, and Molly cracked up laughing. "Okay, WHAT is the first thing you need to do before you open your script?" asked Aunt Sherry.

"Pray," Molly answered. "I'll pray and then we can get started reading our script."

Remember, Bible study should always begin with prayer. We need to ask God to help us understand what the Bible says and to direct us by His Holy Spirit, so we can make sure we understand His Word and handle it accurately.

All right! Now that we have prayed, did you know that Daniel is a book in the Bible that is both historical and prophetic? Since you study history in school, you know that history is about people and events. Prophecy is when God reveals to us what is going to happen in the future. Season One (*You're a Brave Man, Daniel!*) of our new television series will focus on the historical events in Daniel 1–6, while Season Two

(*Fast-Forward to the Future*) on Daniel 7–12 will show us what is going to happen in the future. Pretty cool, huh?

Now that you know what our television series is going to be about, let's scan our script to make sure we have just the right location to begin taping our television series. Your script is the Observation Worksheets located at the back of this book. These pages have the Bible text printed out for you to use.

5 Turn to page 134. Read Daniel 1:1-2. To discover the setting and characters for our new television series, we need to ask the 5 W's and an H. WHAT are the 5 W's and an H? They are the WHO, WHAT, WHERE, WHEN, WHY, and HOW questions.

OBSERVATION WORKSHEETS

DANIEL 1-6

(page 134)

6 **Chapter 1**

1 In the third year of the reign of Jehoiakim king of Judah, Nebuchadnezzar king of Babylon came to Jerusalem and besieged it.

2 The Lord gave Jehoiakim king of Judah into his hand, along with some of the vessels of the house of God; and he brought them to the land of Shinar, to the house of his god, and he brought the vessels into the treasury of his god.

3 Then the king ordered Ashpenaz, the chief of his officials, to

1. Since this book is both a historical and prophetic book, (page 9) asking WHO is very important. Asking WHO helps you find out:

   WHO are the main characters?

   WHO is this prophecy about?

   WHO is involved?

2. WHAT helps you understand:

   WHAT are the main events taking place?

   WHAT is God telling you?

3. In any historical event, WHERE is very important. And in prophecy it is also important to know WHERE it happens.

   WHERE helps you learn:

   WHERE did something happen?

   WHERE did they go?

   WHERE was this said?

   When we discover a WHERE, we double-underline the WHERE in green.

Guided Instruction

5 Turn to page 9 and review the inductive study questions.

6 Turn to page 134 and read Daniel 1:1-2 to answer the questions on page 10-13.

Guided Instruction

Daniel 1:1 WHEN does this scene take place? (b.) the third year of the reign of Jehoiakim

WHO are two of the characters in our script? Jehoiakim, king of Judah and Nebuchadnezzar, king of Babylon.

---

10   WEEK ONE

4. WHEN tells us about time. We mark it with a green clock 🕐 or a green circle like this: ◯.

WHEN tells us:

WHEN did this event happen or WHEN is it going to happen?

WHEN is so very important in history and prophecy. It helps us follow the order of events.

5. Looking at history, WHY asks questions like:

WHY did this event happen?

Looking at prophecy, WHY asks:

WHY is God telling us this is going to happen?

6. HOW lets you figure out things like:

HOW did something happen?

HOW did the people react to what happens?

HOW is something going to happen in the future?

HOW does it come to pass?

Now read your script and ask those 5 W's and an H.

Daniel 1:1 WHEN does this scene take place? Draw a green clock or green circle over this time phrase in Daniel 1:1 on page 134. Then circle the correct answer below.

a. the first year of the reign of Jehoiakim

(b.) the third year of the reign of Jehoiakim

c. the sixth year of the reign of Jehoiakim

WHO are two of the characters in our script?

_____Jehoiakim_____, king of _____Judah_____ and

Nebuchadnezzar, king of _____Babylon_____

Look at the chart "The Rulers and Prophets of Daniel's Time," and circle the names of these two rulers.

THE RULERS AND PROPHETS OF DANIEL'S TIME

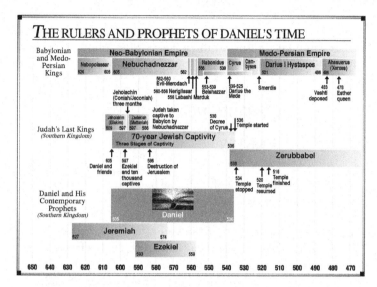

So WHERE are our two kings from?

Daniel 1:1 WHAT is the location of Jehoiakim, the king of Judah? WHERE does Nebuchadnezzar come to?

J e r u s a l e m

Daniel 1:1-2 WHERE is King Nebuchadnezzar from?

King of B a b y l o n, the land of _____ Shinar

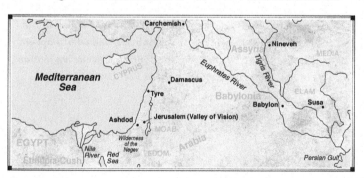

Guided Instruction

Daniel 1:1 WHAT is Jehoiakim's location? WHERE does Nebuchadnezzar come to?
J e r u s a l e m

Daniel 1:1-2 WHERE is King Nebuchadnezzar from? King of B a b y l o n, the land of Shinar

Guided Instruction

7 Read the "Production Manager's Notes" on page 12.

To learn more about the special location King Nebuchadnezzar is from, take a look at the notes of Miss Anna, the production manager, below.

 7

PRODUCTION MANAGER'S NOTES

BABYLON means "gate of God" and is one of the most important cities in the ancient world.

Babylon is located east of the Euphrates River, 56 miles south of present-day Baghdad in Iraq. It is in the fertile plain of Mesopotamia between two rivers: the Tigris and the Euphrates. It lies near the Garden of Eden, near the cradle of civilization.

The first mention of this ancient city in the land of Shinar is found in Genesis 10–11. In Genesis 11, the people of Babel (Babylon) sin by wanting to make a name for themselves instead of having God rule over them. From the beginning of time, this city has been in opposition to God.

Keep your eyes and ears open because Babylon not only plays an important part in history, but it will also play a part in the future. You can study more about Babylon and what happens to it in the future by studying the Book of Revelation in Max and Molly's Bible adventure A SNEAK PEEK INTO THE FUTURE.

Daniel 1:1 WHAT did Nebuchadnezzar come to Jerusalem to do?

_____ **To besiege Jerusalem** _____

Daniel 1:2 WHO wins this battle?

_____ **King Nebuchadnezzar** _____

Daniel 1:2 WHO gave King Jehoiakim, the king of Judah, into King Nebuchadnezzar's hand? WHO was in control?

_____ **God** _____

Wow! Are you surprised to see that God gave Jehoiakim into King Nebuchadnezzar's hand? WHY would God allow His chosen people, the sons of Israel, to be taken captive by their enemies? One way we can find out is by looking at some other passages of Scripture. This is called *cross-referencing.*

8 Look up and read Deuteronomy 28:1-7.

Deuteronomy 28:1 WHAT did the children of Israel need to do to be set high above all the nations of the earth?

"_____ **Obey** _____ the LORD your God, being careful to _____ **do** _____ all His **commandments** ."

Deuteronomy 28:7 WHAT would happen to Israel's enemies if Israel obeyed?

Israel's enemies will be _____ **defeated** _____.

Read Deuteronomy 28:15,25.

Deuteronomy 28:25 WHAT would happen if Israel did not obey? WHAT would the Lord cause the children of Israel to be?

_____ **Defeated** _____ before your _____ **enemies** _____

Guided Instruction

Daniel 1:1 WHAT did Nebuchadnezzar come to Jerusalem to do? To besiege Jerusalem

Daniel 1:2 WHO wins the battle? King Nebuchadnezzar

Daniel 1:2 WHO gave King Jehoiakim, the king of Judah, into King Nebuchadnezzar's hand? God

8 Read the selected scripture in Deuteronomy to answer the questions.

Deuteronomy 28:1-7 WHAT did the children of Israel need to do to be set high above all the nations of the earth? "Obey the Lord your God, being careful to do all His commandments."

Deuteronomy 28:7 WHAT will happen to Israel's enemies if Israel obeys? Israel's enemies will be defeated.

Deuteronomy 28:25 WHAT would happen if Israel did not obey? WHAT would the Lord cause the children of Israel to be? Defeated before your enemies

Guided Instruction

9 Read the questions on page 14 and elicit discussion. Have students respond independently.

10 Read the text on pages 14-15.

---

14   WEEK ONE

Wow! Look at HOW important it was to God that the children of Israel obey Him! They would defeat their enemies if they obeyed, but if they disobeyed, then they would be defeated.

9 HOW about you? Do you think God expects you to obey Him?

_____

WHY? _____

HOW are you going to know what God wants you to do? Would studying the Bible help you to know what God expects? HOW would studying the Bible help you?

_____

HOW much do you obey God? Circle one of the answers below.

    a. all the time   b. a lot of the time

    c. sometimes   d. not very often

WHICH answer should you circle? Write it out below:

_____

10   Now that you have thought about what you do and what you should do, why don't you go to God and ask Him to help you change anything that you need to change, to help you obey Him?

Way to go! You have done some awesome research today. You went straight to God's book, the book of truth. You saw that there are two kings: the king of Judah who is king over God's chosen people, and the king of Babylon, king over a very wicked city who defeats the king of Judah and takes some of the sons of Israel into captivity.

You also saw by looking at other passages of Scripture that God told His people as long as they obeyed Him, they would defeat their enemies. Does that mean the sons of Israel didn't obey God and His commandments since King Nebuchadnezzar takes God's chosen people into captivity? You'll find out tomorrow as you continue the research for our new television series. But before you leave the set today, you need to discover your memory verse for this week.

Did you know that the original language the Bible was written in was Hebrew with some Aramaic in the Old Testament, and Koine Greek in the New Testament? Since the Book of Daniel is written in both the Hebrew and Aramaic languages, we thought it would be fun if you discovered this week's verse by using a fun made-up language that kids like to use called "Pig Latin."

There are different ways to write Pig Latin depending on if a word begins with one consonant, multiple consonants, or a vowel. If a word begins with a single consonant, you take the consonant off the front of the word and put it at the end of the word, adding *ay* after it (such as, if I wanted to say *Daniel* in Pig Latin, I would say *anielday*).

Now if a word begins with two or more consonants, you would take the group of consonants off the front of the word and add them to the end, and then add *ay* to the end of the word. For an example, the word *choice* would become *oicechay*. And if a word starts with a vowel, you just add *ay* to the end of the word. For example, the word *up* would become *upay*.

Solve this week's verse by looking at the words on the next page that are in Pig Latin and writing the real word for this fun made-up language underneath each blank. Then find the reference for your verse in Daniel 1. Practice this verse by saying it in both Pig Latin and English three times in a row, three times today!

Guided Instruction

Guided Instruction

11 Unscramble the Pig Latin message on page 16. This is your memory verse.

"<u>But</u> <u>Daniel</u> <u>made</u> <u>up</u> <u>his</u> <u>mind</u> <u>that</u> <u>he</u> <u>would</u> <u>not</u> <u>defile</u> <u>himself</u> <u>with</u> <u>the</u> <u>king's</u> <u>choice</u> <u>food</u>, <u>or</u> <u>with</u> <u>the</u> <u>wine</u> <u>which</u> <u>he</u> <u>drank</u>; <u>so</u> <u>he</u> <u>sought</u> <u>permission</u> <u>from</u> <u>the</u> <u>commander</u> <u>of</u> <u>the</u> <u>officials</u> <u>that</u> <u>he</u> <u>might</u> <u>not</u> <u>defile</u> <u>himself</u>."

Daniel 1:<u>8</u>

Practice saying the memory verse three times, three times a day.

Say it to a partner.

---

16   WEEK ONE

11

utbay	anielDay	ademay	upay	ishay	indmay
<u>But</u>	<u>Daniel</u>	<u>made</u>	<u>up</u>	<u>his</u>	<u>mind</u>

atthay	ehay	ouldway	otnay	efileday	imselfhay
<u>that</u>	<u>he</u>	<u>would</u>	<u>not</u>	<u>defile</u>	<u>himself</u>

ithway	ethay	ingskay	oicechay	oodfay	oray
<u>with</u>	<u>the</u>	<u>king's</u>	<u>choice</u>	<u>food,</u>	<u>or</u>

ithway	ethay	ineway	ichwhay	ehay	ankdray;
<u>with</u>	<u>the</u>	<u>wine</u>	<u>which</u>	<u>he</u>	<u>drank;</u>

osay	ehay	oughtsay	ermissionpay	omfray	ethay
<u>so</u>	<u>he</u>	<u>sought</u>	<u>permission</u>	<u>from</u>	<u>the</u>

ommandercay	ofay	ethay	officialsay	atthay	ehay
<u>commander</u>	<u>of</u>	<u>the</u>	<u>officials</u>	<u>that</u>	<u>he</u>

ightmay	otnay	efileday	imselfhsay.
<u>might</u>	<u>not</u>	<u>defile</u>	<u>himself.</u>

Daniel 1: <u>8</u>

You did it! We are so proud of you!

(page 16)

ON THE SET OF ISRAEL

12 "Look at that, Molly! Isn't that set amazing?" Max asked as they walked onto the set with Aunt Sherry. "It looks just like the pictures I have seen of ancient Jerusalem."

Aunt Sherry told the kids, "This is the set where we will shoot our opening scene as King Nebuchadnezzar comes up against King Jehoiakim to besiege the city."

"Will we start filming today?" Max asked Aunt Sherry.

Welcome to Babylon…or Modern-Day Iraq   17

"Not yet. We need to finish casting our characters. But first you and Molly need to find out WHAT the sons of Israel did that caused God to let them be taken into captivity. After you do your research, you can help me, Miss Leslie, and Mr. Preston, the casting director, finish casting."

"All right!" Molly exclaimed. "Let's get started."

Don't forget to pray! Let's find out WHAT the children of Israel did that caused God to allow them to be defeated. Start by looking at the production manager's notes on the nation of Israel.

13 **PRODUCTION MANAGER'S NOTES**

The beginning of the nation of Israel is found in the Book of Genesis as God promises to make Abram (Abraham) a great nation in Genesis 12. This nation is to come through his son, Isaac (Genesis 17:19; Genesis 21:12), and through Isaac's son Jacob (Genesis 28).

In Genesis 35:10, God changes Jacob's name to Israel. Jacob (Israel) has 12 sons, whose descendants are known as the 12 tribes of Israel, God's chosen people.

In 1 Kings, because of King Solomon's divided heart, God divides the 12 tribes of Israel into two kingdoms: the north and the south.

The northern kingdom of Israel is made up of 10 tribes of Israel. They settle in the north and claim Samaria as their capital.

The southern kingdom of Judah is made up of the remaining two tribes of Israel, Benjamin and Judah, who keep Jerusalem as their capital.

God has a special message for you today. Ask Him to clear your focus and enable you to understand His Word.

12 Turn to page 16 and read "On the Set of Israel."

13 Read the "Production Manager's Notes" on page 17 to place you in the historical context.

Guided Instruction

Which kingdom has King Nebuchadnezzar come after? ⓑ **the southern kingdom of Judah whose capital is Jerusalem**

18   WEEK ONE

So which kingdom has King Nebuchadnezzar come after?

a. the northern kingdom of Israel whose capital is Samaria

ⓑ. the southern kingdom of Judah whose capital is Jerusalem

14   Look at Daniel 1:1 to see if you got the right answer. Let's solve the crossword puzzle below to find out what happens to both of these kingdoms. We need to see if either kingdom does what God tells them to do.

18

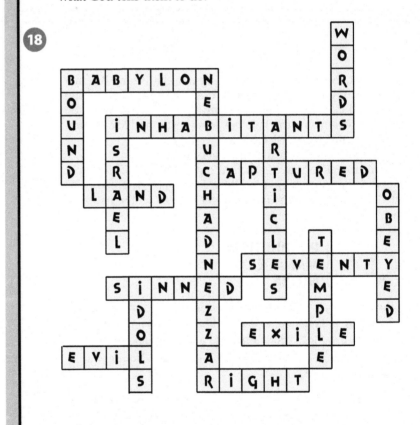

15 First let's find out what happens to the northern kingdom of Israel. Look up and read 2 Kings 17:5-7,12.

2 Kings 17:6 WHAT did the king of Assyria do?

1. (Across) He ___captured___ Samaria and carried

2. (Down) ___Israel___ away into

3. (Across) ___exile___ to Assyria.

WHY did this happen?

2 Kings 17:7 Because the sons of Israel had

4. (Across) ___sinned___ against the Lord their God.

2 Kings 17:9 The sons of Israel did things secretly which were not

5. (Across) ___right___ against the Lord their God.

2 Kings 17:12 They served

6. (Down) ___idols___.

16 Now let's complete our puzzle by looking at the southern kingdom of Judah that King Nebuchadnezzar has come after. Look up and read 2 Chronicles 36:5-7.

2 Chronicles 36:5 WHAT did King Jehoiakim do?

7. (Across) He did ___evil___ in the sight of the Lord his God.

2 Chronicles 36:6 WHAT happened when King Nebuchadnezzar came up against King Jehoiakim?

King Nebuchadnezzar

8. (Down) ___bound___ him with bronze chains to take him to

9. (Across) ___Babylon___.

Guided Instruction

14 Read the selected scripture verses on pages 19-20 to complete the crossword puzzle on page 18 (TG page 22).

15 Read 2 Kings 17:5-12 and analyze each one to answer the questions.

2 Kings 17:6 WHAT did the king of Assyria do?

1. (Across) He captured Samaria and carried

2. (Down) Israel away into

3. (Across) exile to Assyria.

WHY did this happen? 2 Kings 17:7 Because the sons of Israel had

4. (Across) sinned against the Lord their God.

2 Kings 17:9 The sons of Israel did things secretly which were not

5. (Across) right against the Lord their God.

2 Kings 17:12 They served

6. (Down) idols.

16 Read 2 Chronicles 36:5-7 and analyze each one to answer the questions.

2 Chronicles 36:5 WHAT did King Jehoiakim do?

7. (Across) He did evil in the sight of the Lord his God.

2 Chronicles 36:6 WHAT happened when King Nebuchadnezzar came up against King Jhoiakim?

King Nebuchadnezzar

8. (Down) bound him with bronze chains to take him to

Guided Instruction

9. (Across) Babylon.

2 Chronicles 36:7 WHAT else did King Nebuchadnezzar bring to Babylon?

10. (Down) Some of the articles of the house of the Lord

WHERE did he put these articles of God?

11. (Down) In his temple at Babylon

🔢17 Read Jeremiah 25:8-11 and analyze each one to answer the questions.

"You have not

12. (Down) obeyed

13. (Down) My words."

Jeremiah 25:9 WHAT is the Lord going to do?

14. (Down) "I will send to Nebuchadnezzar king of Babylon, My servant, and bring them against this

15. (Across) land and against its

16. (Across) inhabitants."

Jeremiah 25:11 HOW long will they be in captivity and serve the king of Babylon?

17. (Across) seventy years

🔢18 Use the underlined words to complete the crossword puzzle on page 18 (TG page 22).

🔢19 Read the rest of the text on pages 20-22.

---

20   WEEK ONE

2 Chronicles 36:7 WHAT else did King Nebuchadnezzar bring to Babylon?

10. (Down) Some of the ____articles____ of the house of the Lord

WHERE did he put these articles of God?

11. (Down) In his ____temple____ at Babylon

⑰ Look up and read Jeremiah 25:8-11.

Jeremiah 25:8 WHAT did the Lord of hosts tell them?

"You have not

12. (Down) __obeyed__

13. (Down) My ____words____."

Jeremiah 25:9 WHAT is the Lord going to do?

14. (Down) "I will send to ____Nebuchadnezzar____ king of Babylon, My servant, and bring them against this

15. (Across) ____land____ and against its

16. (Across) ____inhabitants____."

Jeremiah 25:11 HOW long will they be in captivity and serve the king of Babylon?

17. (Across) ____seventy____ years

⑲   Can you believe it? Both of these kingdoms disobey God and are taken into captivity. The northern kingdom of Israel is taken into captivity by Assyria in 772 BC. Then the southern kingdom of Judah is taken into captivity by the Babylonians in three different sieges of Jerusalem, which begin in 605 BC with King Jehoiakim. Looking at both of these kingdoms, does God do exactly what He says He will do?

Yes! God always does what He says He will do. God told the nation of Israel in Deuteronomy 28 that if they obeyed God, being careful to do all His commandments, they would be set high above all the nations of the earth and their enemies would be defeated. But as we have seen today, they didn't obey. They didn't listen to God. Instead they chose to do things God said were not right. They chose to serve idols instead of worshiping God. They sinned against God. James 4:17 says, *"Therefore, to one who knows the right thing to do and does not do it, to him it is sin."*

That's why we're studying God's Word—so that we can know and do what God says is right. HOW can we apply WHAT we learned about these two kingdoms to our lives? Let's look at how you spend your time.

20 WHAT are some of the things that you do every week? Do you play sports, talk with friends on the Internet, or play a musical instrument? Name some of the things you do:

_____

_____

Do you talk to God during the day? Do you have time to study your Bible? Do you let God talk to you through the Bible about His commandments?

_____

_____

Israel got into trouble for worshiping idols. Idols are not just statues. Idols are anything in your life that you put *before* God, like watching television, playing sports, or playing video games. WHAT are some of the things that you put before God?

_____

_____

These activities and things we listed aren't wrong unless you put them in God's place. That's why we want you to check yourself to see how you're spending your time. If God is God, then He should be number one in your life!

22   WEEK ONE

Way to go! We are so proud of you for studying and applying God's Word! Now don't forget to practice your memory verse. This verse shows you something very important about our main character's character. Tomorrow we will find out what happens after King Nebuchadnezzar captures the city.

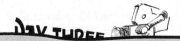

DAY THREE

Guided Instruction

20 Read and discuss the personal questions on page 21. Have students respond independently to each personal reflection.

Pull out your memory verse card and practice saying it three times with a friend.

Guided Instruction

Do you realize what a blessing it is to dig into the Word? Ask God to give you clear understanding of His lesson today.

21 Turn to page 22 and read "Casting Call."

22 Read the selected verses, Daniel 1:1-7, to answer the questions.

(page 22)

21

CASTING CALL

It's great to have you back on the set! Now that you have the historical background information for our television series, are you ready to help Aunt Sherry, Miss Leslie, and Mr. Preston finish casting our characters? Great! Also, Mr. Andy, the prop master, needs some help gathering the props for our first scene. Grab your script (page 134) and let's head back to Daniel 1. Don't forget to talk to God!

22 Read Daniel 1:1-7 and ask those 5 W's and an H.

(page 134)

Chapter 1

1 In the third year of the reign of Jehoiakim king of Judah, Nebuchadnezzar king of Babylon came to Jerusalem and besieged it.

2 The Lord gave Jehoiakim king of Judah into his hand, along with some of the vessels of the house of God; and he brought them to the land of Shinar, to the house of his god, and he brought the vessels into the treasury of his god.

3 Then the king ordered Ashpenaz, the chief of his officials, to bring in some of the sons of Israel, including some of the royal family and of the nobles,

4 youths in whom was no defect, who were good-looking, showing intelligence in every branch of wisdom, endowed with understanding and discerning knowledge, and who had ability for serving in the king's court; and he ordered him to teach them the literature and language of the Chaldeans.

5 The king appointed for them a daily ration from the king's choice food and from the wine which he drank, and appointed that they should be educated three years, at the end of which they were to enter the king's personal service.

6 Now among them from the sons of Judah were Daniel, Hananiah, Mishael and Azariah.

7 Then the commander of the officials assigned new names to them; and to Daniel he assigned the name Belteshazzar, to

(page 135)

Hananiah Shadrach, to Mishael Meshach and to Azariah Abednego.

Daniel 1:2 WHEN Jerusalem is besieged WHAT is taken from the house of God? WHAT props do we need? *(page 22)*

Vessels

WHERE are these vessels taken?

To the land of Shinar; to the house and treasury of King Jehoiakim's god

23 Think about how God would feel about His holy vessels being taken from His house into the house of a false god. Does King Nebuchadnezzar have respect for God's holy vessels? **No.**

Even though it looks like Nebuchadnezzar and his gods are

Welcome to Babylon…or Modern-Day Iraq   23

more powerful since he has taken the city and the holy vessels, WHO did we see was in control in Daniel 1:2? **God**

Remember: Even when things look bad, God is still in control.

Now that we have our props, let's cast our characters.

Daniel 1:3 WHOM did King Nebuchadnezzar order the chief of his officials, Ashpenaz, to bring in?

Some of the **sons** of **Israel**

Daniel 1:3 WHOM did some of these include?

Some of the **royal** **family** and of the **nobles**

Daniel 1:4 Describe these sons of Israel.

They were "y **o u t h** s…who were **good**-**looking**, showing **intelligence**, endowed with **understanding** and discerning **knowledge**."

Daniel 1:4 WHAT did the king order Ashpenaz to teach them?

The literature and language of the Chaldeans

Guided Instruction

Daniel 1:2 When Jerusalem is besieged, WHAT is taken from the house of God? WHAT props do we need? Vessels

WHERE are these vessels taken? To the land of Shinar; to the house and treasury of King Jehoiakim's god

23 Read the next question and reflect on the meaning. Does King

Did Nebuchadnezzar respect God's holy vessels? No.

WHO do we see was in control in Daniel 1:2? God

CAST the characters.

Daniel 1:3 WHOM did King Nebuchadnezzar order the chief of his officials, Ashpenaz, to bring in? Some of the sons of Israel

Daniel 1:3 WHOM did some of these include? Some of the royal family and of the nobles

Daniel 1:4 Describe these sons of Israel. They were "y o u t h s… who were good-looking, showing intelligence, endowed with understanding and discerning knowledge."

Daniel 1:4 WHAT did the king order Ashpenaz to teach them? The literature and language of the Chaldeans

Guided Instruction

Daniel 1:5 WHAT did the king appoint them a daily ration of? His choice food and wine

Daniel 1:5 HOW long were they to be educated? Three years

WHAT was to happen to them after they were educated? They would enter the king's personal service.

Daniel 1:6 WHO are the four main characters taken from the sons of Judah? Daniel, Hananiah, Mishael, and Azariah

Daniel 1:7 WHAT did the commander of the officials assign to these sons of Israel? New names

24 WRITE out each one of the new names next to their original name.

Daniel: Belteshazzar
Hananiah: Shadrach
Mishael: Meshach
Azariah: Abed-nego

25 Read the meaning of each new name and answer the question:

---

24   WEEK ONE

Daniel 1:5 WHAT did the king appoint them a daily ration of?

His choice food and wine

Daniel 1:5 HOW long were they to be educated?

Three years

WHAT was to happen to them after they were educated?

They would enter the king's personal service.

Did you notice that each one of these youths (teenagers) who are taken into captivity are considered the best of the best? They are smart, athletic, handsome, the finest in the land of Israel. They are taken from their homes, their language, and their beliefs and put in the king's royal school to be taught the king's language and beliefs.

Daniel 1:6 WHO are the four main characters taken from the sons of Judah?

Daniel, Hananiah, Mishael, and Azariah

Daniel 1:7 WHAT did the commander of the officials assign to these sons of Israel?

New names

24 Write out each one of the new names next to their original name.

Daniel: Belteshazzar   Hananiah: Shadrach
Mishael: Meshach   Azariah: Abed-nego

WHY were these four teenagers given new names? Did you know that in Bible times a person's name was very important because it showed the person's character and identity? Let's look

25 at the meaning of these four guys' Hebrew names. *Daniel* means

"God is my judge," *Hananiah* means "Jehovah has been gracious" (Jehovah and Yahweh are Hebrew names for God), *Mishael* means "Who is what God is" (in other words, there is nobody like God), and *Azariah* means "Yahweh has helped." In each one of these boy's Hebrew names, we see the name of God.

Now look at the meaning of their new Babylonian names. *Belteshazzar* means "Bel will protect," *Shadrach* means "inspired of Aku," *Meshach* means "belonging to Aku," and *Abed-nego* means "servant of Nego." Each one of these Babylonian names has a reference to a false god. Bel, Nego, and Aku were all names of the false gods of the Babylonians.

Since names showed a person's character and identity, do you think that King Nebuchadnezzar changed these youths' names to change their identity, to show his ownership over them now that they have been taken into captivity? ___**Yes**___

26 Daniel was about 15 years old when he was taken from his home into captivity. Can you imagine not only being taken from your home, but also being taken to a foreign city, a new school, having your name changed, and not even understanding the language?

HOW would you feel? Would you be scared, anxious, or confused? Would you think God didn't love you, had forgotten you, or couldn't protect you? Would you continue to trust and follow God in spite of what had happened to you? Write out HOW you would feel and WHAT you would do.

_____

_____

_____

Guided Instruction

Are the new names intended to show the king's ownership of the youths?
Yes

26 Read the next two questions and elicit a discussion. Have each student respond independently.

Guided Instruction

27 Read the text below the last question. Reflect on the meaning of being removed from home, family, and friends.

Practice saying the memory verse.

---

26   WEEK ONE

HOW would it feel to have the people who captured you brag that their god was stronger than your God, especially since you know it's not true?

---

27   HOW will Daniel and his friends handle being taken to a foreign country of a heathen king who doesn't know God and respect His holy vessels? Any hopes and dreams they had for their future have just been shattered. They are no longer free; they will never return home to see their families again. Will they become angry over their circumstances? Will they bend under the pressure? Will they change what they believe, or will they continue to love and trust God in spite of everything that has happened to them? We'll find out. You have done an awesome job at casting our characters! Don't forget to practice your memory verse.

some job at casting our characters! Don't forget to
your memory verse.

(page 26)

DAY FOUR

❷❽ CAMERA CHECK

"Hey, Max, why don't you and Molly come help me get these props ready for our camera check?" Mr. Andy asked as Max and Molly arrived on the set of Babylon.

"Sure, Mr. Andy. We'd love to help," Max said. "Oh man, these props are making me hungry. Look at all these great things to eat." Molly laughed. "So, Max, which would you rather have: the king's choice food or these yummy vegetables?"

Before Max could answer, Aunt Sherry walked onto the set. "The king's table looks great. Are you ready for us to do our camera check, Andy?"

"I think we're ready," replied Andy.

How about you? Let's grab our scripts and make sure Mr. Andy has all the props for our next scene. Pray and then turn to

---

Welcome to Babylon…or Modern-Day Iraq   27

page 135. Read Daniel 1:8-21. Ask the 5 W's and an H to prepare for our camera check.

Observation Worksheets   135

Hananiah Shadrach, to Mishael Meshach and to Azariah Abednego.

❷❾ 8 But Daniel made up his mind that he would not defile himself with the king's choice food or with the wine which he drank; so he sought permission from the commander of the officials that he might not defile himself.

9 Now God granted Daniel favor and compassion in the sight of the commander of the officials,

10 and the commander of the officials said to Daniel, "I am afraid of my lord the king, who has appointed your food and your drink; for why should he see your faces looking more haggard than the youths who are your own age? Then you would make me forfeit my head to the king."

11 But Daniel said to the overseer whom the commander of

DAY FOUR

Ask God to open your mind to understand His Word today.

❷❽ Turn to page 26 and read "Camera Check."

❷❾ Read Daniel 1:8-21 and analyze each verse to answer the questions on pages 27-29.

Guided Instruction

(page 135)

11 But Daniel said to the overseer whom the commander of the officials had appointed over Daniel, Hananiah, Mishael and Azariah,

12 "Please test your servants for ten days, and let us be given some vegetables to eat and water to drink.

13 "Then let our appearance be observed in your presence and the appearance of the youths who are eating the king's choice food; and deal with your servants according to what you see."

14 So he listened to them in this matter and tested them for ten days.

15 At the end of ten days their appearance seemed better and they were fatter than all the youths who had been eating the king's choice food.

136   *Observation Worksheets*

16 So the overseer continued to withhold their choice food and the wine they were to drink, and kept giving them vegetables.

17 As for these four youths, God gave them knowledge and intelligence in every branch of literature and wisdom; Daniel even understood all kinds of visions and dreams.

18 Then at the end of the days which the king had specified for presenting them, the commander of the officials presented them before Nebuchadnezzar.

19 The king talked with them, and out of them all not one was found like Daniel, Hananiah, Mishael and Azariah; so they entered the king's personal service.

20 As for every matter of wisdom and understanding about which the king consulted them, he found them ten times better than all the magicians and conjurers who were in all his realm.

21 And Daniel continued until the first year of Cyrus the king.

(page 27)

for our camera check.

Daniel 1:8 WHAT did Daniel do?

Daniel __made__   __up__ his m_i_ _n_ _d_.

Do you know what it means to make up your mind? Making up your mind is making a decision in your heart. It's like drawing a line in the sand and saying, "This is what I believe. This is what I will do. I will not cross over this line."

Daniel 1:8 WHAT did Daniel make up his mind about?

__He would not defile himself with the king's food and__ wine.

Daniel 1:8 WHAT did Daniel seek?

He sought __permission__ from the __commander__ of the __officials__ that he might not __defile__ himself.

28   WEEK ONE

them what is clean and okay to eat, and what is unclean and not okay to eat. If you want to read about these laws, you can find them in Leviticus 11 and Deuteronomy 14. Daniel knows God's law and chooses to honor God by what he eats and drinks.

Daniel 1:9 WHAT does God grant Daniel?

__Favor and compassion__

Daniel 1:10 WHY was the commander of the officials afraid to change Daniel's food and drink?

__He was afraid of the king.__

Daniel 1:11-12 WHAT did Daniel ask the overseer to do?

"To __test__ your servants for __ten__ days"

Daniel 1:12 WHAT did Daniel ask for them to be given to eat and drink?

__Vegetables and water__

Guided Instruction

Daniel 1:8 WHAT did Daniel do? Daniel made up his m i n d.

Daniel 1:8 WHAT did Daniel make up his mind about? He would not defile himself with the king's food and wine.

Daniel 1:8 WHAT did Daniel seek? He sought permission from the commander of the officials that he might not defile himself.

Daniel 1:9 WHAT does God grant Daniel? Favor and compassion

Daniel 1:10 WHY was the commander of the officials afraid to change Daniel's food and drink? He was afraid of the king.

Daniel 1:11-12 WHAT did Daniel ask the overseer to do? "To test your servants for ten days"

Daniel 1:12 WHAT did Daniel ask for them to be given to eat and drink? Vegetables and water

Guided Instruction

Daniel 1:15 WHAT happened after they were tested for 10 days? Their appearance seemed better than all the youth who ate the king's food.

Daniel 1:11-17 WHO took the test? b. Four of the youths: Daniel, Hananiah, Mishael, and Azariah

Daniel 1:17 WHAT did God give these four youths? Knowledge and intelligence in every branch of literature and wisdom

Daniel 1:17 WHAT did Daniel understand? Visions and dreams

Daniel 1:18-20 WHAT happened to them when they were presented before Nebuchadnezzar? Not one was found like Daniel, Hananiah, Mishael, and Azariah; so they entered the king's personal service.

Daniel 1:17 HOW did these guys get to be so smart? God gave them knowledge and intelligence.

Daniel 1:21 HOW long did Daniel continue? Until the first year of Cyrus the king

(page 28)

Daniel 1:15 WHAT happened after they were tested for 10 days?
Their appearance seemed better than all the youth who ate the king's food.

Daniel 1:11-17 WHO took the test—all of the youths or just four of the youths (Daniel and his three friends)? Circle the correct answer.

a. All of the youths

(b.) Four of the youths: Daniel, Hananiah, Mishael, and Azariah

Daniel 1:17 WHAT did God give these four youths?
Knowledge and intelligence in every branch of literature and wisdom

Welcome to Babylon…or Modern-Day Iraq   29

Daniel 1:17 WHAT did Daniel understand?
Visions and dreams

Daniel 1:18-20 WHAT happened to them when they were presented before Nebuchadnezzar?

Not one was found like Daniel, Hananiah, Mishael, and Azariah; so they entered the king's personal service.

HOW did these guys get to be so smart? Look back at Daniel 1:17 if you missed it.
God gave them knowledge and intelligence.

Daniel 1:21 HOW long did Daniel continue?
Until the first year of Cyrus the king

(page 29)

Wow! Daniel and his friends are teenagers far away from home in a wicked city, where no one will ever know if they give in to temptation and follow the crowd. But instead of giving in when they are tested, they do what God says is right.

30 HOW about you? WHAT would you do if you knew no one would find out? Would you lie to your parents about where you are going and whom you are going to be with? Would you drink, smoke, inhale something to make you feel different, or take drugs? Or would you dare to go against the crowd and do what God says is right? Write out what you would do:

31 _____

_____

_____

Look at how God honored these four teenagers' decision to do what He says is right. Their appearances were better than the other youths, and God gave them knowledge, intelligence,

30   WEEK ONE

and wisdom. They each entered into the king's personal service. Pretty cool, huh?

All right! Our camera check is finished and we are ready to start filming. Tomorrow we will get a close-up of God and one of our awesome teenagers.

Guided Instruction

30 Elicit discussion about the next questions: HOW about you?

31 After a time of reflection, have students write independent responses.

Guided Instruction

This last day students will reflect on their personal character and integrity. Ask God to help you lead them through reflection and application.

32 Turn to page 30 and read "Zooming In."

33 Review Pronouns on pages 30-31.

34 Turn to page 134 and write key word markings over the title and/or make a key word bookmark by copying them on an index card of piece of paper.

(page 30)

32

ZOOMING IN

"All right, quiet on the set. We are ready to roll," Aunt Sherry called out. "Camera One, I want you to zoom in right after the opening sequence. Let's count it down, and…action."

Are you ready to "zoom in" and take a closer look at God and Daniel? Great! Don't forget to ask God for His help. Pull out your script and let's get a close-up on both God and Daniel.

One way you can uncover clues about the main events and characters in the Book of Daniel is to mark them in a special way so you can get a closer look at them. Today we are going to "zoom in" on our scripts and mark every place we see *God* and *Daniel.* We also need to mark each pronoun that refers to either God or Daniel. WHAT are pronouns? Check out Max and Molly's notes below.

33

Pronouns

Pronouns are words that take the place of nouns. A noun is a person, place, or thing. A pronoun stands in for a noun! Here's an example: "Molly and Max are excited about helping on the new television series on Daniel. They can't wait to discover what happens to Daniel now that he has been taken into captivity." The word *they* is a pronoun because it takes the place of Molly and Max's names in the

(page 31)

second sentence. It is another word we use to refer to Molly and Max.

Watch for these other pronouns when you are marking people's names:

I	you	he	she
me	yours	him	her
mine		his	hers
we	it		
our	its		
they	them		

Now that you know what pronouns are, turn to your Observation Worksheets on page 134. Read Daniel 1 and mark *God* and *Daniel* in a special way, just like we have listed below:

God (draw a purple triangle and color it yellow)

34

Daniel (color it blue)

All right! Now look in your script at each verse where you

OBSERVATION WORKSHEETS
DANiEL 1-6

(page 134)

(35) **Chapter 1**

1 In the third year of the reign of Jehoiakim king of Judah, Nebuchadnezzar king of Babylon came to Jerusalem and besieged it.

2 The Lord gave Jehoiakim king of Judah into his hand, along with some of the vessels of the house of God; and he brought them to the land of Shinar, to the house of his god, and he brought the vessels into the treasury of his god.

3 Then the king ordered Ashpenaz, the chief of his officials, to bring in some of the sons of Israel, including some of the royal family and of the nobles,

4 youths in whom was no defect, who were good-looking, showing intelligence in every branch of wisdom, endowed with understanding and discerning knowledge, and who had ability for serving in the king's court; and he ordered him to teach them the literature and language of the Chaldeans.

5 The king appointed for them a daily ration from the king's choice food and from the wine which he drank, and appointed that they should be educated three years, at the end of which they were to enter the king's personal service.

6 Now among them from the sons of Judah were Daniel, Hananiah, Mishael and Azariah.

7 Then the commander of the officials assigned new names to them; and to Daniel he assigned the name Belteshazzar, to

---

Observation Worksheets   135

Hananiah Shadrach, to Mishael Meshach and to Azariah Abednego.

8 But Daniel made up his mind that he would not defile himself with the king's choice food or with the wine which he drank; so he sought permission from the commander of the officials that he might not defile himself.

9 Now God granted Daniel favor and compassion in the sight of the commander of the officials,

afraid

Guided Instruction

God (draw a purple triangle and color it yellow)

Daniel (color it blue)

(35) Read Daniel I on page 134 aloud as students follow along. If you are teaching in a classroom and have an overhead projector, make a transparency of your Observation Worksheet for a visual aid. You may want to blow it up to poster size and hang it on a wall and then have your students call each key word out loud as you read it and mark it together—you on the transparency and they in their books. If you're skilled at PowerPoint and have time, you can import an Observation Worksheet then select symbols from PP's palette or elsewhere, color them, place them over the words, and even animate them—bring them in one at a time.

Guided Instruction

(page 135)

of the commander of the officials;

10 and the commander of the officials said to Daniel, "I am afraid of my lord the king, who has appointed your food and your drink; for why should he see your faces looking more haggard than the youths who are your own age? Then you would make me forfeit my head to the king."

11 But Daniel said to the overseer whom the commander of the officials had appointed over Daniel, Hananiah, Mishael and Azariah,

12 "Please test your servants for ten days, and let us be given some vegetables to eat and water to drink.

13 "Then let our appearance be observed in your presence and the appearance of the youths who are eating the king's choice food; and deal with your servants according to what you see."

14 So he listened to them in this matter and tested them for ten days.

15 At the end of ten days their appearance seemed better and they were fatter than all the youths who had been eating the king's choice food.

136   *Observation Worksheets*

16 So the overseer continued to withhold their choice food and the wine they were to drink, and kept giving them vegetables.

17 As for these four youths, God gave them knowledge and intelligence in every branch of literature and wisdom; Daniel even understood all kinds of visions and dreams.

18 Then at the end of the days which the king had specified for presenting them, the commander of the officials presented them before Nebuchadnezzar.

19 The king talked with them, and out of them all not one was found like Daniel, Hananiah, Mishael and Azariah; so they entered the king's personal service.

20 As for every matter of wisdom and understanding about which the king consulted them, he found them ten times better than all the magicians and conjurers who were in all his realm.

21 And Daniel continued until the first year of Cyrus the king.

Chapter 2

(page 31)

36 All right! Now look in your script at each verse where you marked *God* in Daniel 1:2, 9, and 17. Let's find out what you learned about God from each of these verses. We want to make sure our television viewers know the truth about WHO God is and WHAT He does, so that they can get to know Him, too! Make a list of everything you learned about God in the box below.

37

WHAT I Learned About God

Daniel 1:2 **God gave King Jehoiakim over to King Nebuchadnezzar.**

Daniel 1:9 **God granted Daniel favor and compassion in the sight of the commander of the officials.**

Daniel 1:17 **God gave the youth knowledge and intelligence in every branch of literature and wisdom.**

---

32   WEEK ONE

Amazing! Stop and think about WHAT this list shows us about WHO God is, about His power, and about WHAT He can do.

In Daniel 1:2, the Lord gave the outcome of the battle. God is the One who allowed Jerusalem to be defeated by King Nebuchadnezzar and allowed Daniel and the other youths to be taken into captivity. God is the One in control of people. This shows us that God is sovereign. There is absolutely nothing that God doesn't have control over!

In Daniel 1:9, God is the One who got other people to show favor and compassion to Daniel. God loves us! He cares about what happens to us.

In Daniel 1:17, God gave the four youths knowledge, intelligence, and wisdom. What an *awesome* God! Would God do this for you?

Let's make a list on WHAT we know about Daniel by look-

Guided Instruction

36 Read the selected verses to answer the questions.

37 Write what you learned about God from Daniel 1:2, 9, and 17.

WHAT I Learned About God

Daniel 1:2 God gave King Jehoiakim over to King Nebuchadnezzar.

Daniel 1:9 God granted Daniel favor and compassion in the sight of the commander of the officials.

Daniel 1:17 God gave the youth knowledge and intelligence in every branch of literature and wisdom.

Guided Instruction

 Write what you learned about Daniel (see TG page 40.)

WHAT I Learned About Daniel

Daniel 1:6 <u>One of the sons of Judah was taken to Babylon</u>.

Daniel 1:7 <u>Given a new name</u>

Daniel 1:8 <u>Made up his mind not to defile himself with the king's choice food or the wine he drank. He sought permission from the commander of the officials</u>.

Daniel 1:9 <u>He was granted favor and compassion by God</u>.

Daniel 1:17 <u>He understood all kinds of visions and dreams. He was given knowledge and intelligence in every branch of literature and wisdom</u>.

Daniel 1:19 <u>Not one was found like Daniel, Hananlah, Mishael, and Azariah; so they entered the king's personal service</u>.

Daniel 1:21 <u>He continued until the first year of Cyrus the King</u>.

(page 32)

for you?

Let's make a list on WHAT we know about Daniel by looking at where we marked his name on our script. Put the facts in the box below.

> **38**
>
> **WHAT I Learned About Daniel**
>
> **Daniel 1:6** One of the sons of Judah was taken to Babylon.
>
> **Daniel 1:7** Given a new name
>
> **Daniel 1:8** Made up his mind not to defile himself with the king's choice food or the wine he drank. He sought permission from the commander of the officials.
>
> **Daniel 1:9** He was granted favor and compassion by God.
>
> **Daniel 1:17** He understood all kinds of visions and dreams. He was given knowledge and intelligence in every branch of literature and wisdom.
>
> **Daniel 1:19** Not one was found like Daniel, Hananlah, Mishael, and Azariah; so they entered the king's personal service.
>
> **Daniel 1:21** He continued until the first year of Cyrus the King.

Wow! Would you like to be like Daniel? Let's do a character profile on Daniel to see if you could play Daniel's part.

CHARACTER PROFILE

Daniel	Me

Daniel has faith.

Faith is believing God; it is taking Him at His Word. Faith is when you believe what God says in the Bible, and it shows by the way you act. You decide to do what God says is right. Daniel believes God. He does what God says is right. He chooses to trust God in a very hard and difficult situation.

Do you have faith?

Have you placed your trust in Jesus Christ?

Yes _____   No _____

Do you do what God says is right? Name one thing you do that shows you love and trust God. Here are some examples: Do you read your Bible every day? Do you obey your parents? Do you want to please God? Do you listen and pay attention to His Word? Do you believe God means what He says and act like it? Do you ask God to help you not to lie, steal, gossip, or talk about other kids?

Write out one way that shows you have faith:

_____

_____

Daniel has integrity.

Integrity is doing the right thing when no one is looking. Integrity is being trustworthy and sincere. A person with integrity has the highest standards and is honest, pure, and consistent.

Look at Daniel's integrity. He has the highest standards. Daniel makes up his mind not to defile himself. He keeps himself pure. He sets himself

Do you have integrity?

Can your parents trust you to obey them when they are not around? Have you made up your mind to live God's way, to keep yourself pure? Name a standard that you have set for yourself, like waiting to get married before having sex, or deciding not to drink alcohol.

_____

WHAT would you do if you spent

Guided Instruction

39 Work closely with the students to complete the Character Profile on pages 33-35.

The profile makes students reflect on their current integrity and character so they can determine what and how to improve.

Take each "Character Profile" of Daniel, one-at-a-time. Read each one aloud as students follow along. Then read the comparable items under the ME column. Ask students to reflect inwardly and write independent responses on the line provided.

Guided Instruction

Daniel	39	Me

apart from the world he is living in. Daniel dares to be different.

the night with friends and they are watching things on TV or looking at things on the Internet that are wrong? Would you go along, or would you say, "This doesn't please God. I can't look at or be a part of this"? Write out what you would do:

_____

_____

WHAT if Mom or Dad were looking over your shoulder while you were on the Internet? Would you slip into code language, or do you have such integrity that Mom and Dad could read what you are writing?

_____

Daniel has courage.

Courage is boldness; it is taking a stand and doing what you know is right even though you are afraid. Daniel took a stand, even though he didn't know what would happen to him if he went against the king's command and refused the food from his table.

Do you have courage?

Will you be brave like Daniel and stand up for what you know is right, even if it means you will not be cool or popular and that others will laugh at you? Write out one way you will have courage. Write out what you will do when someone tries to get you to do the wrong thing:

_____

_____

_____

_____

Guided Instruction

Daniel	**Me**

Daniel has humility.

Humility is a lack of pride. Humility is knowing our weaknesses as well as our strengths. Daniel humbled himself before the commander of the officials. He asked for permission not to eat the king's food and wine. He submitted himself to his authority. He was respectful. How about you?

Are you humble?

Do you submit yourself to those who are in authority over you?

_____Yes _____ No

Are you respectful? HOW do you treat your parents and your teachers?

_____

HOW do you talk about them to your friends when they aren't around to hear you?

_____

Daniel has self-discipline.

Self-discipline is learning to train and control your behavior. It is being able to turn away from temptation. It is choosing to do right even when it is hard and difficult. It is sticking with something, even though it is dull and boring. It requires determination and sacrifice. How tempting do you think it was for Daniel to look at the king's choice food and not eat it? Daniel disciplined himself. He did not give in to temptation. He chose to do what was right, even though it was hard and difficult.

Do you have self-discipline?

WHAT do you eat? Do you choose healthy foods or junk foods?

_____

Training yourself to eat healthy foods, playing sports or a musical instrument, memorizing God's Word, saving for something you want to buy, doing your homework, and cleaning your room without being asked are all things that take self-discipline. Name one thing you do that shows you have self-discipline:

_____

_____

Guided Instruction

40 Read the rest of the text on page 36.

Take out your memory verse card and say it to a partner.

You have been diligent throughout this study. God sees and is pleased.

If you are a classroom teacher you may want to give your students a quiz on their memory verse. There is also a quiz on Week One on page 153 to check memory and understanding.

If you are a Sunday School teacher this is a great time to review the whole week by playing a game like *The Matching Game* on page 163 or *M&M® Draw* on page 164.

---

40 36   WEEK ONE

What an *awesome* teenager! Look at how Daniel's character is revealed in these hard and difficult circumstances. Daniel dares to be different—he trusts God. Dare to be different. Ask God to help you be a Daniel in your world. Don't follow the crowd to be cool and popular. Make up your mind to honor and live for God!

How do you think Daniel developed such strong character? Could it be because he started learning God's Word when he was younger, like you? That's why we are so proud of you! You are learning to be like Daniel.

Don't forget to say your memory verse out loud to a grown-up this week. Ask the person to tell you something that he or she made up their mind about. Next week we will film a very interesting dream. WHO has this dream, and WHAT does it mean?

2

A KING'S DREAM

DANIEL 2

It's great to have you back on the set. Last week as we began filming our television series, we saw King Nebuchadnezzar besiege Jerusalem, and God allowed the sons of Israel to be taken into captivity. Four awesome teenagers stand out from the rest because they make up their minds to trust God and do what He says is right.

Pretty amazing! Did you make up your mind to be brave like Daniel and do what God says is right? Way to go! WHAT will we discover this week? Let's head back to the set to find out.

DAY ONE

41

LIGHTS, CAMERA, ACTION...

"That looks so cool," Molly said to Max as they walked on set and she spotted King Nebuchadnezzar's bedroom.

"I bet Aunt Sherry is opening the scene with Nebuchadnezzar dreaming," Max replied.

"You're right, Max." Aunt Sherry smiled as she greeted the kids. "That's exactly how we're opening up. Sam, stop bothering Mr. Hunter. Quit pulling on his pant leg. He's one of our gaffers."

37

Guided Instruction

WEEK 2

DAY ONE

Ask God to lead you to understand His special message today. Remember, He is always with you. Study His Word to draw closer to Him.

41 Turn to page 37 and read "Daniel 2" and "Lights, Camera, Action..."

Guided Instruction

42 Review the importance of noticing Key Words.

---

38   WEEK TWO

"Cool it, Sam," Max told Sam as he picked him up. "Sorry about that, Mr. Hunter. What does a gaffer do?"

"It's okay, Max. A gaffer works with the lighting. He's an electrician or a lighting technician. Sam just isn't sure about all these lights and wires."

"Are you and Molly ready to get to work on your scripts," Aunt Sherry asked, "while Mr. Hunter makes sure the lighting is just right?"

Move it a little to the left...

"We sure are," answered Molly. "I'll pray. Then we can mark our scripts so we'll be ready when the action starts."

Don't forget to talk to God! Now you're going to mark key words on your Observation Worksheets.

42 What are *key words?* Key words are words that pop up more than once. They are called key words because they help unlock the meaning of the chapter or book that you are studying and give you clues about what is most important in a passage of Scripture.

- Key words are usually used over and over again.
- Key words are important.
- Key words are used by the writer for a reason.

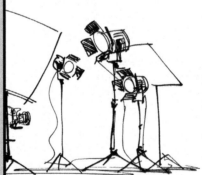

Once you discover a key word, you need to mark it in a special way using a special color or symbol so that you can immediately spot it in Scripture.

Look at the key-word box on the next page. These are the key words for Daniel 2 that you will mark this week. You may also want to make a bookmark for these key words so that you can see them at a glance as you mark them on your Observation Worksheets.

So let's get started. Make your key-word bookmark by taking an index card and writing the key words listed in the box below, as well as how you are going to mark them on your Observation Worksheets.

Then turn to page 136. Read Daniel 2:1-12 and mark your key words in these verses on your Observation Worksheets.

Key Words for Daniel 2

God (draw a purple triangle and color it yellow, or just color it yellow)

Daniel (color it blue)

Nebuchadnezzar (color it orange)

dream (vision) (draw a blue cloud around it)

mystery (box it in orange and color it green)

kingdom (draw a purple crown and color it blue)

---

(43)

Don't forget to mark your pronouns! And mark anything that tells you WHERE by double-underlining the WHERE in green. Mark anything that tells you WHEN by drawing a green clock or green circle like this: ◯ .

Now let's find out what upsets King Nebuchadnezzar and keeps him from sleeping in our opening scene. Ask those 5 W's and an H.

(page 136)

21 And Daniel continued until the first year of Cyrus the king.

Chapter 2

(44) 1 Now in the second year of the reign of Nebuchadnezzar, Nebuchadnezzar had dreams; and his spirit was troubled and his sleep left him.

2 Then the king gave orders to call in the magicians, the conjurers, the sorcerers and the Chaldeans to tell the king his dreams. So they came in and stood before the king.

3 The king said to them, "I had a dream and my spirit is anxious to understand the dream."

4 Then the Chaldeans spoke to the king in Aramaic: " O king,

Guided Instruction

(43) Copy the key word markings on page 39 to your bookmark and above the title, "Daniel 2" on page 136.

God (draw a purple triangle and color it yellow)

Daniel (color it blue)

Nebuchadnezzar (color it orange)

Dream (vision) (draw a blue cloud around it)

Mystery (box it in orange and color it green)

Kingdom (draw a purple crown and color it blue)

WHERE (double-underline words that denote place in green)

WHEN (draw a green clock over words that denote time)

(44) After copying the key word markings, read Daniel 2:1-12 on page 136 aloud using your Observation Worksheet visual aid as students follow along and call out each key word. Then mark them together as we noted on page 37.

(page 40)

Guided Instruction

Observation Worksheets   137

live forever! Tell the dream to your servants, and we will declare the interpretation."

5 The king replied to the Chaldeans, " The command from me is firm: if you do not make known to me the dream and its interpretation, you will be torn limb from limb and your houses will be made a rubbish heap.

6 "But if you declare the dream and its interpretation, you will receive from me gifts and a reward and great honor; therefore declare to me the dream and its interpretation."

7 They answered a second time and said, "Let the king tell the dream to his servants, and we will declare the interpretation."

8 The king replied, "I know for certain that you are bargaining for time, inasmuch as you have seen that the command from me is firm,

9 that if you do not make the dream known to me, there is only one decree for you. For you have agreed together to speak lying and corrupt words before me until the situation is changed; therefore tell me the dream, that I may know that you can declare to me its interpretation."

10 The Chaldeans answered the king and said, "There is not a man on earth who could declare the matter for the king, inasmuch as no great king or ruler has ever asked anything like this of any magician, conjurer or Chaldean.

11 "Moreover, the thing which the king demands is difficult, and there is no one else who could declare it to the king except gods, whose dwelling place is not with mortal flesh."

---

138   Observation Worksheets

12 Because of this the king became indignant and very furious and gave orders to destroy all the wise men of Babylon.

(page 39)

Daniel 2:1 WHEN is this happening? (Did you remember to put a green clock over this time phrase?)

In the **second** year of the reign of **Nebuchadnezzar**

---

40   WEEK TWO

Daniel 2:1 WHAT troubles Nebuchadnezzar's spirit and causes him to lose sleep? He has a ____**dream**____.

Daniel 2:2 WHAT does King Nebuchadnezzar want the magicians, the conjurers, the sorcerers, and the Chaldeans to tell the king?

The dreams

Daniel 2:4 WHAT language did the Chaldeans speak to the king?

a. Hebrew   b. Aramaic

Do you remember from Week One that Daniel was written in both the Hebrew and Aramaic languages? Daniel 1 is written in the Hebrew language, which is the language of the sons of Israel (the Jews). Daniel 2–7 is written in Aramaic, which was the language of Nebuchadnezzar and the Gentile nations.

Daniel 2:4 WHAT did the Chaldeans want the king to do?

Tell them the dreams

Daniel 2:5 WHAT would the king do to them if they did not tell both the dream and the interpretation?

They would be torn limb from limb and their homes would be destroyed.

Daniel 2:8-9 WHY did the king want them to tell both? WHAT did the king think they would do if he told them the dream?

They would agree together and **speak** **lying** and **corrupt words** until the situation is changed.

Read the selected verses to answer the questions.

Daniel 2:1 WHEN is this happening?
In the **second** year of the reign of **Nebuchadnezzar**

Daniel 2:1 WHAT troubles Nebuchadnezzar's spirit and causes him to lose sleep? He has a **dream**.

Daniel 2:2 WHAT does King Nebuchadnezzar want the magicians, the conjurers, the sorcerers, and the Chaldeans to tell the king? **The dreams**

Daniel 2:4 WHAT language did the Chaldeans speak to the king? **b. Aramaic**

Daniel 2:4 WHAT did the Chaldeans want the king to do? **Tell them the dreams**

Daniel 2:5 WHAT would the king do to them if they did not tell both the dream and the interpretation? **They would be torn limb from limb and their homes would be destroyed.**

Daniel 2:8-9 WHY did the king want them to tell both? WHAT did the king think they would do if he told them the dream? **They would agree together and speak lying and corrupt words until the situation was changed.**

Guided Instruction

Daniel 2:10-11 Can they tell him both the dream and the interpretation? <u>No</u>.

WHO do they say can interpret the dream? <u>The gods</u>

Daniel 2:12 HOW does the king react? <u>He becomes indignant and furious.</u>

Daniel 2:12 WHAT orders does the king give? <u>To destroy all the wise men</u>

A King's Dream   41

Daniel 2:10-11 Can they tell him both the dream and the interpretation? ___No.___

WHO do they say can interpret the dream?

The gods

Daniel 2:12 HOW does the king react?

He becomes indignant and furious.

Daniel 2:12 WHAT orders does the king give?

To destroy all the wise men

Wow! Can you believe this? King Nebuchadnezzar is so angry that he gives orders to destroy all the wise men of Babylon. WHOM do these orders include? We'll find out as we continue filming this exciting episode tomorrow!

But before we leave today, we need to discover our new memory verse. Become the script person to make sure Daniel gets his lines just right in our second episode that blesses the God of heaven. Look at the words inside Daniel's thoughts on the next page. As the script person, you need to place each word where it needs to go on our cue card that follows.

Then look up Daniel 2 and find the reference for this verse. Don't forget: You need to learn these lines and practice them three times in a row, three times every day to remind you of WHO God is and how to praise Him for what He has done for you!

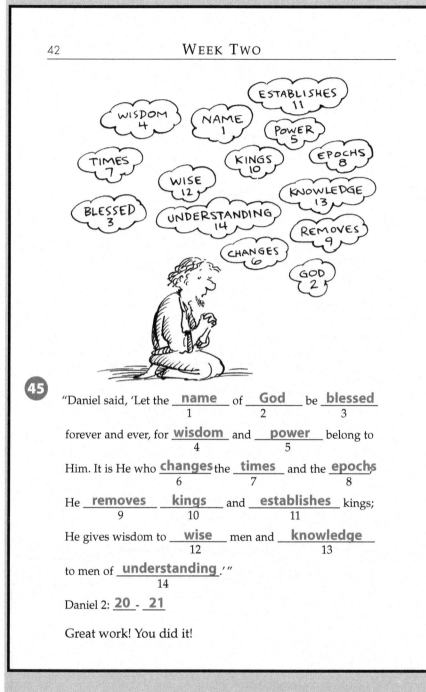

42   WEEK TWO

45 "Daniel said, 'Let the __name__ of __God__ be __blessed__
                        1   2   3

forever and ever, for __wisdom__ and __power__ belong to
                        4   5

Him. It is He who __changes__ the __times__ and the __epochs__/
                    6   7   8

He __removes__ __kings__ and __establishes__ kings;
      9   10   11

He gives wisdom to __wise__ men and __knowledge__
                      12   13

to men of __understanding__.'"
            14

Daniel 2: __20__ - __21__

Great work! You did it!

Guided Instruction

45 Turn to page 42 and place each word in the cloud where it needs to go to complete the memory verse. Then copy this verse to an index card.

"Daniel said, 'Let the <u>name</u> of <u>God</u> be <u>blessed</u> forever and ever, for <u>wisdom</u> and <u>power</u> belong to Him. It is He who <u>changes</u> the <u>times</u> and the <u>epochs</u>. He <u>removes</u> <u>kings</u> and <u>establishes</u> kings; He gives wisdom to <u>wise</u> men and <u>knowledge</u> to men of <u>understanding</u>.'"
Daniel 2:<u>20-21</u>

Practice reading the verse three times in a row each day until you have it memorized.

Guided Instruction

DAY TWO

The next verses are exciting. You will see how Daniel and his friends relied on God's protection and faithfulness in order to avoid being put to death.

Ask God to move in your spirit mightily so you will have a close relationship with Him. Ask Him to clearly speak to you today.

46 Turn to page 43 and read "Scan the Script!"

Review key words on page 39.

God (draw a purple triangle and color it yellow)

Daniel (color it blue)

Nebuchadnezzar (color it orange)

Dream (vision) (draw a blue cloud around it)

Mystery (box it in orange and color it green)

Kingdom (draw a purple crown and color it blue)

WHERE (double-underline words that denote place in green)

WHEN (draw a green clock over words that denote time)

A King's Dream   43

DAY TWO

46

SCAN THE SCRIPT!

"Watch out, Mr. Hunter," Max called as he and Molly walked onto the set. "Here comes Sam!"

Mr. Hunter laughed as he caught Sam. "Oh no you don't, boy. I have heard all about your famous face-licking. You come over here and hop up into your chair. Good boy. Ahhh, you got me!"

"Thanks, Mr. Hunter," Max laughed. "He got so excited when he heard your voice that he broke away. He has decided that you're his new friend."

"I'm glad to hear that, except for the face-licking that comes with it. Are you and Molly ready to find out what happens now that King Nebuchadnezzar is furious with all the wise men of Babylon?"

"We sure are," Molly answered.

"Great! Then why don't you pray, and you can get started marking your script while we do a final check on our lighting?"

All right! Now that you have talked to God, turn to page 39 for a list of your key words to mark or use your key-word bookmark.

Start scanning your script. Turn to page 138. Read Daniel 2:13-18 and mark your key words in these verses on your Observation Worksheets.

We are ready to film. Ask those 5 W's and an H and watch

(page 39)

Key Words for Daniel 2

God (draw a purple triangle and color it yellow, or just color it yellow)

Daniel (color it blue)

Nebuchadnezzar (color it orange)

dream (vision) (draw a blue cloud around it)

mystery (box it in orange and color it green)

kingdom (draw a purple crown and color it blue)

47 13 So the decree went forth that the wise men should be slain, and they looked for Daniel and his friends to kill them.

14 Then Daniel replied with discretion and discernment to Arioch, the captain of the king's bodyguard, who had gone forth to slay the wise men of Babylon;

15 he said to Arioch, the king's commander, "For what reason is the decree from the king so urgent?" Then Arioch informed Daniel about the matter.

16 So Daniel went in and requested of the king that he would give him time, in order that he might declare the interpretation to the king.

17 Then Daniel went to his house and informed his friends, Hananiah, Mishael and Azariah, about the matter,

18 so that they might request compassion from the God of heaven concerning this mystery, so that Daniel and his friends would not be destroyed with the rest of the wise men of Babylon.

19 Then the ~~mystery was revealed to Daniel in a night vision.~~

(page 138)

Observation Worksheets.

We are ready to film. Ask those 5 W's and an H and watch the action unfold.

(page 43)

Daniel 2:13 WHO is included in those orders to destroy all the wise men of Babylon? WHO else is going to be killed?

Daniel, Hananiah, Mishael, and Azariah

44   WEEK TWO

Daniel 2:14 HOW does Daniel reply to the king's bodyguard who comes to kill them?

With ____**discretion**____ and ____**discernment**____

Daniel 2:16 WHAT does Daniel do?

He asks the king for time to interpret his dream.

Just look at our awesome young man! Here he is about to be put to death, and yet he has the courage to ask the king to give him time so he can tell him the dream.

Daniel 2:17 WHAT does Daniel do?

He tells Hananiah, Mishael, and Azariah about the order.

Daniel 2:18 WHAT does Daniel ask his friends to do?

To pray that he and his friends would not be destroyed

They are

Guided Instruction

47 Turn to page 138 and read Daniel 2:13-18 aloud using your Observation Worksheet visual aid as students follow along and call out each key word. Then mark them together as we noted on page 37.

Refer to the selected verses to answer the questions on pages 43-44.

Daniel 2:13 WHO is included in those orders to destroy all the wise men of Babylon? WHO else is going to be killed? Daniel, Hananiah, Mishael, and Azariah

Daniel 2:14 HOW does Daniel reply to the king's bodyguard who comes to kill them? With discretion and discernment

Daniel 2:16 WHAT does Daniel do? He asks the king for time to interpret his dream.

Daniel 2:17 WHAT does Daniel do? He tells Hananiah, Mishael, and Azariah about the order.

Daniel 2:18 WHAT does Daniel ask his friends to do? To pray that he and his friends would not be destroyed

Guided Instruction

48 Elicit a discussion about the next two questions and have students respond independently.

Do you have faith like Daniel's? WHAT do you do in a crisis?

God is the only one who can control people. WHAT will you do the next time you're scared and in trouble?

Pull out your memory verse card and practice reading it with a friend three times. Can you say it by memory yet?

(page 44)

WHAT is this that our four young men are doing? They are praying. They are asking God for compassion. To have compassion is to feel someone else's sorrow and suffering, to help them. Daniel and his friends are asking God to help them, to give them the answer to the mystery. Daniel has faith. He has so much confidence in God that he tells the king that he will give the meaning of his dream.

48   Do you have a faith like Daniel's? _____

WHAT do you do when you are in a crisis? Do you run to God who has all the answers, or do you run to your friends for their answers?

_____
_____

A King's Dream   45

Think about this for a minute. If you run to your friends instead of God, do you think your friends are smarter than God? Can they tell you what is going to happen in the future? Can they control kings? Only God knows the future. He is the only One who has the power to control people and events. Write out what you will do the next time you are scared and in trouble:

_____
_____

What will happen to Daniel and his three friends? Will God answer their prayers? Will the king change his mind about killing all the wise men? Hang in there! We'll find out! Don't forget to practice your memory verse.

(page 45)

DAY THREE

(49) ## SPOTLIGHT ON THE GOD OF HEAVEN

Yesterday was pretty intense as we left Daniel and his three friends requesting compassion from God to solve the mystery and give Daniel the answer to the king's dream. Are you ready to find out what happens? Then grab those scripts and shine the spotlight on the God of heaven. Turn to page 138. Read Daniel 2:19-30 and mark the key words listed on page 39 for these verses on your Observation Worksheets or use your key-word bookmark.

Don't forget to mark your pronouns! And mark anything that tells you WHERE by double-underlining the WHERE in green. Mark anything that tells you WHEN by drawing a green clock 🕐 or green circle like this: ◯.

Now be a gaffer and shine God's spotlight. Ask the 5 W's and an H questions.

(page 138)

(50) 19 Then the mystery was revealed to Daniel in a night vision. Then Daniel blessed the God of heaven;

20 Daniel said,

"Let the name of God be blessed forever and ever,

For wisdom and power belong to Him.

21 "It is He who changes the times and the epochs;

He removes kings and establishes kings;

He gives wisdom to wise men

Observation Worksheets   139

And knowledge to men of understanding.

22 "It is He who reveals the profound and hidden things;

He knows what is in the darkness,

And the light dwells with Him.

23 "To You, O God of my fathers, I give thanks and praise,

For You have given me wisdom and power;

Even now You have made known to me what we requested of You,

For You have made known to us the king's matter."

24 Th...

Guided Instruction

DAY THREE

It's time to stand up and cheer! You are witnessing God's approachability. You, too, can come directly to God with every need. Ask Him to lead you to clear understanding of His Word.

(49) Turn to page 45 and read "Spotlight on the God of Heaven."

Review key words on page 39.

God (draw a purple triangle and color it yellow)

Daniel (color it blue)

Nebuchadnezzar (color it orange)

Dream (vision) (draw a blue cloud around it)

Mystery (box it in orange and color it green)

Kingdom (draw a purple crown and color it blue)

WHERE (double-underline words that denote place in green)

WHEN (draw a green clock over words that denote time)

(50) Turn to page 138 and read Daniel 2:19-30 aloud using your Observation Worksheet visual aid as students follow along and call out each key word. Then mark them together as we noted on page 37.

Guided Instruction

(page 139)

24 Therefore, Daniel went in to Arioch, whom the king had appointed to destroy the wise men of Babylon; he went and spoke to him as follows: "Do not destroy the wise men of Babylon! Take me into the king's presence, and I will declare the interpretation to the king."

25 Then Arioch hurriedly brought Daniel into the king's presence and spoke to him as follows: "I have found a man among the exiles from Judah who can make the interpretation known to the king!"

26 The king said to Daniel, whose name was Belteshazzar, "Are you able to make known to me the dream which I have seen and its interpretation?"

27 Daniel answered before the king and said, "As for the mystery about which the king has inquired, neither wise men, conjurers, magicians nor diviners are able to declare it to the king.

28 "However, there is a God in heaven who reveals mysteries, and He has made known to King Nebuchadnezzar what

140   *Observation Worksheets*

will take place in the latter days. This was your dream and the visions in your mind while on your bed.

29 "As for you, O king, while on your bed your thoughts turned to what would take place in the future; and He who reveals mysteries has made known to you what will take place.

30 "But as for me, this mystery has not been revealed to me for any wisdom residing in me more than in any other living man, but for the purpose of making the interpretation known to the king, and that you may understand the thoughts of your mind.

WEEK TWO

46

Daniel 2:19 Does God answer Daniel and his friends' prayers? WHAT does it say in verse 19?

"The __mystery__ was __revealed__ to __Daniel__ in a __night__ __vision__."

Look at Daniel 2:23. WHAT does Daniel say?

"For You have __given__ me __wisdom__ and __power__; even now You have made __known__ to me what we __requested__ of You, for You have __made__ __known__ to us the __king's__ matter."

Isn't that *awesome!* Daniel and his friends trusted God, and God gives the answer. When you don't know what to do, when you need an answer, why don't you do what Daniel did? Ask God. Seek help from Him. God is the Revealer of mysteries. He has the answers that you need!

Daniel 2:19-23 WHAT does Daniel do when he receives his answer?

Daniel __blessed__ the God of heaven.

Aren't these verses wonderful? They tell us so much about WHO God is! Make a list in the box below of all the things you learned about God in Daniel 2:19-23.

What I Learned About God

Daniel 2:19 God revealed the mystery. God is the God of heaven.

Daniel 2:20 Name blessed. Wisdom and power belong to God.

Daniel 2:21 God changes times; removes or establishes kings; and gives wisdom to wise men.

Daniel 2:22 God reveals profound and hidden things.

Daniel 2:23 God gave Daniel wisdom and power and made known the king's matter.

Guided Instruction

Read the selected verses to answer the questions on pages 46-47.

Daniel 2:19 Does God answer Daniel and his friends' prayers? WHAT does it say in verse 19? "The <u>mystery</u> was <u>revealed</u> to <u>Daniel</u> in a <u>night vision</u>."

Daniel 2:23 WHAT does Daniel say? "For You have <u>given</u> me <u>wisdom</u> and <u>power</u>; even now You have made <u>known</u> to me what we <u>requested</u> of You, for You have <u>made known</u> to us the <u>king's</u> matter."

Daniel 2:19-23 WHAT does Daniel do when he receives his answer? Daniel <u>blessed</u> the God of heaven.

List things that you learned about God in Daniel 2:19-23.

What I Learned About God

Daniel 2:19: <u>God revealed the mystery. God is the God of heaven</u>.

Daniel 2:20: <u>Name blessed. Wisdom and power belong to God.</u>

Daniel 2:21: <u>God changes times; removes or establishes kings; and gives wisdom to wise men</u>.

Daniel 2:22: <u>God reveals profound and hidden things</u>.

Daniel 2:23: <u>God gave Daniel wisdom and power and made known the king's matter</u>.

Guided Instruction

51 Notice HOW Daniel and his friends handle another scary situation.

Daniel 2:24 WHAT does Daniel tell Arioch after he received his answer from God? "Do not <u>destroy</u> the <u>wise men</u> of Babylon! Take me into the <u>king's</u> <u>presence</u> and I will declare the <u>interpretation</u>."

Daniel 2:25-28 WHO did Daniel tell the king had revealed the mystery of the dream? <u>God</u>

Daniel 2:28-29 WHAT is God making known to King Nebuchadnezzar through this dream? <u>What will happen in the future</u>

A King's Dream   47

Just look at all you have discovered today! Our second episode in our television series opens with a very upset king who is disturbed over a dream that none of his wise men can interpret. So he decides to kill all the wise men, including Daniel and his three friends who are still in training in King Nebuchadnezzar's school.

51 HOW do Daniel and his friends handle another scary situation? They run to God and ask for His answer, and God gives it. Wow!

Daniel 2:24 WHAT does Daniel tell Arioch after he received his answer from God?

"Do not __destroy__ the ___wise___ ___men___ of Babylon! Take me into the __king's__ __presence__, and I will declare the __interpretation__."

Daniel 2:25-28 WHO did Daniel tell the king had revealed the mystery of the dream?

__God__

What does this show us about Daniel? Daniel is humble. He gives God the glory. He doesn't take the credit for himself.

Daniel 2:28-29 WHAT is God making known to King Nebuchadnezzar through this dream?

__What will happen in the future__

Isn't that amazing! God is going to show this king who doesn't have a relationship with Him what is going to happen in the future! God is a God who reveals the profound and hidden things.

WHAT is this king's dream and WHAT does it mean? We'll find out as we continue to shoot our second episode in this exciting new series.

48   WEEK TWO

52 **ZOOMING IN: WHAT'S THE KING'S DREAM?**

You did a great job yesterday as you focused the spotlight on God and watched as He answered Daniel's prayer. Today we are ready to shoot a very important scene as we zoom in close to get our first look at King Nebuchadnezzar's dream. Don't forget to pray!

Turn to page 140. Read Daniel 2:31-35 and mark your key words for these verses on your Observation Worksheets using the list on page 39 or your key-word bookmark.

Don't forget to mark your pronouns! And mark anything that tells you WHERE by double-underlining the WHERE in green.

(page 140)

53 31 "You, O king, were looking and behold, there was a single great statue; that statue, which was large and of extraordinary splendor, was standing in front of you, and its appearance was awesome.

32 "The head of that statue was made of fine gold, its breast and its arms of silver, its belly and its thighs of bronze,

33 its legs of iron, its feet partly of iron and partly of clay.

34 "You continued looking until a stone was cut out without hands, and it struck the statue on its feet of iron and clay and crushed them.

35 "Then the iron, the clay, the bronze, the silver and the gold were crushed all at the same time and became like chaff from the summer threshing floors; and the wind carried them away so that not a trace of them was found. But the stone that struck the statue became a great mountain and filled the whole earth.

36 "This was the dream; now we will tell its interpretation

Guided Instruction

WOW! Isn't this exciting? You are about to find out how God shows the future by using a statue.

Ask God to give you clear understand of this message today.

52 Turn to page 48 and read "Zooming in: What's the King's Dream?"

Review key words on page 39.

God (draw a purple triangle and color it yellow)

Daniel (color it blue)

Nebuchadnezzar (color it orange)

Dream (vision) (draw a blue cloud around it)

Mystery (box it in orange and color it green)

Kingdom (draw a purple crown and color it blue)

WHERE (double-underline words that denote place in green)

WHEN (draw a green clock over words that denote time)

53 Turn to page 140 and read Daniel 2:31-35 aloud using your Observation Worksheet visual aid as students follow along and call out each key word. Then mark them together as we noted on page 37.

Guided Instruction

Read the selected verses to answer the questions on pages 48-50.

Daniel 2:31 WHAT did King Nebuchadnezzar dream about? <u>A great statue</u>

Daniel 2:32 WHAT is the head of the statue made of? <u>Fine gold</u> **(color the head on page 49 this color)**

WHAT are the breast and arms made of? <u>Silver</u> **(color the arms and the breast)**

WHAT are the belly and the thighs made of? <u>Bronze</u> **(color the belly and the thighs)**

Daniel 2:33 WHAT are the legs made of? <u>Iron</u> **(color the legs)**

(page 48)

Daniel 2:31 WHAT did King Nebuchadnezzar dream about?

A great statue
_____

Look at the picture of this awesome statue on page 49. You're going to color this statue just the way King Nebuchadnezzar dreamed it. Don't worry about the lines out to the side that divide the statue. You will find out what to put on those lines tomorrow.

Daniel 2:32 WHAT is the head of the statue made of?

Fine gold
_____

Color the head this color.

WHAT are the breast and arms made of?

Silver
_____

Color the arms and the breast.

A King's Dream   49

WHAT are the belly and the thighs made of?

Bronze
_____

Color the belly and the thighs.

Daniel 2:33 WHAT are the legs made of?

Iron
_____

Color the legs.

(page 49)

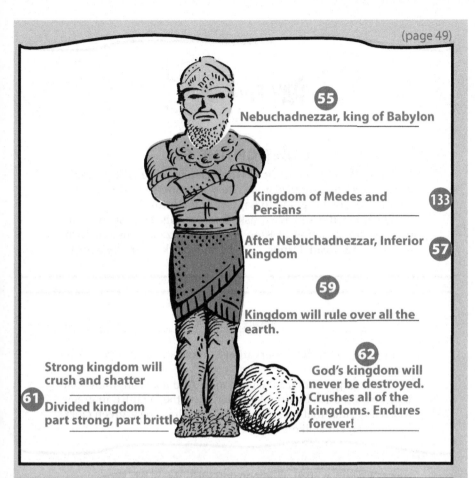

55 Nebuchadnezzar, king of Babylon

133 Kingdom of Medes and Persians

57 After Nebuchadnezzar, Inferior Kingdom

59 Kingdom will rule over all the earth.

Strong kingdom will crush and shatter

61 Divided kingdom part strong, part brittle

62 God's kingdom will never be destroyed. Crushes all of the kingdoms. Endures forever!

Guided Instruction

WHAT are the feet made of? Iron and clay (color the feet.)

Daniel 2:34 WHAT do you learn about the stone? "It was cut out without hands. It struck the statue on its feet of iron and clay and crushed them."

Daniel 2:35 WHAT happened after the stone crushed the feet? The iron, clay, bronze, silver, and gold were crushed at the same time and became like chaff and the wind carried it away so not a trace was found.

WHAT happened to the stone? It became a great mountain and filled the whole earth.

Practice saying the memory verse three times with a friend.

---

50   WEEK TWO

WHAT are the feet made of? **Iron** and **clay** Color the feet.

Daniel 2:34 WHAT do you learn about the stone?
It was **cut** out **without** **hands**.
It **struck** the **statue** on its **feet** of iron and clay and **crushed** them.

Daniel 2:35 WHAT happened after the stone crushed the feet?
The iron, clay, bronze, silver, and gold were crushed at the same time and became like chaff and the wind carried it away so not a trace was found.
WHAT happened to the stone?

It became a **great** **mountain** and filled the **whole** **earth**.

Did you know that mountains in the Bible are sometimes symbols of kingdoms? Pretty amazing! Tomorrow we will find out just what this dream means. Don't forget to praise God by practicing your memory verse. See you on the set!

Guided Instruction

Isn't it awesome how God deals with men? Thank God for the privilege of studying His Word and ask Him to lead you to clear understanding.

Turn to page 81 and read "Quiet on the Set."

Review key words on page 39.

God (draw a purple triangle and color it yellow)

Daniel (color it blue)

Nebuchadnezzar (color it orange)

Dream (vision) (draw a blue cloud around it)

Mystery (box it in orange and color it green)

Kingdom (draw a purple crown and color it blue)

WHERE (double-underline words that denote place in green)

WHEN (draw a green clock over words that denote time)

54 Turn to page 140 and read Daniel 2:36-49 aloud using your Observation Worksheet visual aid as students follow along and call out each key word. Then mark them together as we noted on page 37.

(page 50)

QUIET ON THE SET

Wow! Were you surprised when Daniel revealed the king's dream of an awesome statue? Are you ready to find out what God tells Daniel is going to happen in the future?

Quiet on the set! Let's ask God for His help so we can uncover the meaning of King Nebuchadnezzar's dream. Turn to page 140. Read Daniel 2:36-49 and mark your key words

---

A King's Dream   51

from page 39 on the Observation Worksheets or use your key-word bookmark.

Don't forget to mark the pronouns! And mark anything that tells you WHERE by double-underlining the WHERE in green. Mark anything that tells you WHEN by drawing a green clock or green circle like this: ◯ .

---

54 36 "This was the dream; now we will tell its interpretation before the king.   (page 140)

37 "You, O king, are the king of kings, to whom the God of

Observation Worksheets   141

heaven has given the kingdom, the power, the strength and the glory;

38 and wherever the sons of men dwell, or the beasts of the field, or the birds of the sky, He has given them into your hand and has caused you to rule over them all. **#1** You are the head of gold.

56 39 "After you there will arise another **#2** kingdom inferior to you,

58 then another **#3** third kingdom of bronze, which will rule over all the earth.

60 40 "Then there will be a fourth **#4** kingdom as strong as iron; inasmuch as iron crushes and shatters all things, so, like iron that breaks in pieces, it will crush and break all these in pieces.

(page 141)

41 "In that you saw the feet and toes, partly of potter's clay and partly of iron, it will be a divided kingdom; but it will have in it the toughness of iron, inasmuch as you saw the iron mixed with common clay.

42 "As the toes of the feet were partly of iron and partly of pottery, so some of the kingdom will be strong and part of it will be brittle.

43 "And in that you saw the iron mixed with common clay, they will combine with one another in the seed of men; but they will not adhere to one another, even as iron does not combine with pottery.

44 "In the days of those kings the God of heaven will set up a kingdom which will never be destroyed, and that kingdom will not be left for another people; it will crush and put an end to all these kingdoms, but it will itself endure forever.

142   *Observation Worksheets*

45 "Inasmuch as you saw that a stone was cut out of the mountain without hands and that it crushed the iron, the bronze, the clay, the silver and the gold, the great God has made known to the king what will take place in the future; so the dream is true and its interpretation is trustworthy."

46 Then King Nebuchadnezzar fell on his face and did homage to Daniel, and gave orders to present to him an offering and fragrant incense.

47 The king answered Daniel and said, "Surely your God is a God of gods and a Lord of kings and a revealer of mysteries, since you have been able to reveal this mystery."

48 Then the king promoted Daniel and gave him many great gifts, and he made him ruler over the whole province of Babylon and chief prefect over all the wise men of Babylon.

49 And Daniel made request of the king, and he appointed Shadrach, Meshach and Abed-nego over the administration of the province of Babylon, while Daniel was at the king's court.

Chapter 3

Guided Instruction

Read the selected verses to answer the questions on pages 51-54.

Daniel 2:37-38 WHAT did Daniel tell Nebuchadnezzar? "You, O King, are the king of kings to whom the God of heaven has given the kingdom, the power, the strength, and the glory… [God] has caused you to rule over them all. You are the head of gold."

55 Turn back to page 49 and on the line beside the head of gold write "Nebuchadnezzar, king of Babylon." (TG page 61)

Daniel 2:39 WHAT will there be after King Nebuchadnezzar? Another kingdom that is inferior to King Nebuchadnezzar's.

56 Put a #2 over the "another kingdom" in verse 39 on page 141 (TG page 62).

57 Turn back to page 49 and on the line beside the breast and arms of silver, write "After Nebuchadnezzar, inferior kingdom." (TG page 61)

Daniel 2:39 WHAT do you learn about the third kingdom? A kingdom of bronze, which will rule over all the earth

58 Put a #3 over this third kingdom in verse 39 on page 141 (TG page 62).

59 Turn back to page 49 and on the line beside the legs of iron, write "Kingdom will rule over all the earth." (TG page 61)

Daniel 2:40-43 WHAT do you learn about the fourth kingdom? As strong as iron, it will crush and break all these in pieces. It will be a d i v i d e d kingdom. Some of it will be strong and some of it will be brittle.

(page 51)

Daniel 2:37-38 WHAT did Daniel tell Nebuchadnezzar?

"You, O King, are the **king of kings** to whom the God of heaven has given the ___**kingdom**___, the ___**power**___, the ___**strength**___ and the ___**glory**___… [God] has caused you to ___**rule**___ over them all. You are the ___**head**___ of ___**gold**___."

Isn't it amazing that God would reveal this to King Nebuchadnezzar? Turn back to the picture of your statue on page 49. On the line beside the head of gold write "Nebuchadnezzar, king of Babylon."

Daniel 2:39 WHAT will there be after King Nebuchadnezzar?

___**Another kingdom**___ that is ___**inferior**___ to King Nebuchadnezzar's.

Put a number 2 over this kingdom in your script on page 141 and turn back to your statue on page 49. On the line beside the breast and arms of silver, write "After Nebuchadnezzar, inferior kingdom." Right now we don't know who this kingdom is, just that it will be inferior to Nebuchadnezzar's.

Daniel 2:39 WHAT do you learn about the third kingdom?

A kingdom of ___**bronze**___, which will ___**rule**___ over all the ___**earth**___.

Put a number 3 over this kingdom in your script and turn

back to your statue on page 49. On the line beside the belly and thighs of bronze, write "Kingdom will rule over all the earth."

Daniel 2:40-43 WHAT do you learn about the fourth kingdom?

___**strong**___ as i **r o** n, it will ___**crush**___ and ___**break**___ all these in ___**pieces**___.

It will be a d **i v i d e** d kingdom.

Some of it will be ___**strong**___ and some of it will be ___**brittle**___.

(page 52)

Put a number *4* over this kingdom in your script and turn back to your statue on page 49. On the line beside the legs of iron, write "Strong kingdom will crush and shatter." And by the feet of iron and clay, write "Divided kingdom, part strong, part brittle."

Daniel 2:42-44 WHAT do the toes of the feet represent? Read these verses again. Verse 42 is talking about the toes, and in verse 43 it says "they," referring to the toes, and in verse 44 it says WHAT?

"In the days of those __kings__." The toes are k _i_ _n_ _g_ s!

HOW many toes does a person have? __Ten__ toes

So HOW many kings will there be? _____Ten_____ kings

Daniel 2:44 WHAT is going to happen in those days?

The ____God____ of heaven will set up a ____kingdom____.

Daniel 2:44-45 WHAT do we learn about God's kingdom?

It will never be ____destroyed____, it will not be left for another ____people____, it will ____crush____ and put an ____end____ to all these ____kingdoms____, but it will endure ____forever____.

A King's Dream 53

Daniel 2:34-35 WHAT part of our picture represents God's kingdom? WHAT did we learn about the stone? WHAT did it do?

It s _t_ _r_ _u_ _c_ _k_ the statue on its ____feet____ and c _r_ _u_ _s_ _h_ _e_ _d_ the i _r_ _o_ _n_, the ____clay____, the __bronze__, the ____silver____ and the ____gold____ all at the same time.

Turn back to your statue on page 49. On the line beside the stone, write "God's kingdom will never be destroyed. Crushes all of the kingdoms. Endures forever!"

Aren't you excited? You have just discovered something very, very important. You have just found out WHEN Jesus will come back a second time and set up His kingdom on earth. You know from looking at Daniel 2:44 that God's kingdom will be set up in the days of the ten kings ruling on the earth. Has this happened yet? No. You know that Jesus will not return to set up His kingdom until there are ten kings ruling on the earth.

Guided Instruction

60 Put a **#4** over this kingdom in verse 40 on page 141 (TG page 62).

61 Turn back to page 49 and on the line besides the legs of iron write, "Strong kingdom will crush and shatter" and by the feet of iron and clay, write "Divided kingdom, part strong, part brittle." (TG page 61)

Daniel 2:42-44 WHAT do the toes of the feet represent? "In the days of those kings." The toes are k i n g s!

HOW many toes does a person have? Ten

So, HOW many kings will there be? Ten

Daniel 2:44 WHAT is going to happen in those days? The God of heaven will set up a kingdom.

Daniel 2:44-45 WHAT do we learn about God's kingdom? It will never be destroyed, it will not be left for another people, it will crush and put an end to all these kingdoms, but it will endure forever.

Daniel 2:34-35 WHAT part of our picture represents God's kingdom? WHAT do we learn about the stone? WHAT did it do? It s t r u c k the statue on its feet and c r u s h e d the i r o n, the clay, the bronze, the silver and the gold all at the same time.

62 Turn back to page 49 and on the line beside the stone, write "God's kingdom will never be destroyed. Crushes all of the kingdoms. Endures forever!" (TG page 61)

This is a good time to include a fun activity for the kids. Turn to page 165 and learn how the *Statue Maker* activity can reinforce the key messages of this lesson.

Guided Instruction

Daniel 2:46 WHAT did King Nebuchadnezzar do? He fell on his face and did homage to Daniel and gave orders to present him an offering.

Daniel 2:47 WHAT did Nebuchadnezzar say about Daniel's God? Your God is the God of gods and Lord of kings and a revealer of mysteries.

Daniel 2:48 WHAT happened to Daniel? He was promoted and made ruler of the province of Babylon, and chief prefect over all of the wise men.

Daniel 2:49 WHAT happened to Daniel's friends, Shadrach, Meshach, and Abed-nego? They were appointed over the administration of the province of Babylon, while Daniel was at the king's court.

WHAT is the name of the kingdom that King Nebuchadnezzar is ruling? Babylonian

You are witnessing God's history-making that happened before you were born.

Do you realize how awesome this is?

Thank God for the privilege of seeing how he works in the lives of men.

You have been very diligent through this study. God sees and He is pleased.

If you are a classroom teacher you may want to give your students a quiz on their memory verse. There is also a quiz on Week Two on page 154 to check memory and understanding.

You may *also* want to play *M&M® Draw* on page 164 to review all that the kids have learned in weeks one and two.

(page 53)

His kingdom until there are ten kings ruling on the earth.

Now let's find out WHAT happens to Daniel after he interprets the meaning of this dream.

Daniel 2:46 WHAT did King Nebuchadnezzar do?

He fell on his face and did homage to Daniel and gave orders to present him an offering.

Daniel 2:47 WHAT did Nebuchadnezzar say about Daniel's God?

Your God is the God of gods and Lord of kings and a revealer of mysteries.

Daniel 2:48 WHAT happened to Daniel?

He was promoted and made ruler of the province of Babylon, and chief prefect over all of the wise men.

---

54   Week Two
_____

Daniel 2:49 WHAT happened to Daniel's friends Shadrach, Meshach, and Abed-nego?

They were appointed over the administration of the province of Babylon, while Daniel was at the king's court.

Isn't that fantastic? King Nebuchadnezzar actually bowed before his captive Daniel. Look at how God has taken care of these four awesome young men who put their trust in Him and sought Him for the answers!

Amazing! God has just shown you what is going to happen in the future. You know there will be four kingdoms before Jesus comes back and sets up His kingdom on earth.

Now WHAT is the name of the kingdom that King Nebuchadnezzar is ruling?

Babylonian
_____

HOW many of these kingdoms have already happened today, at our time in history? You'll find out as we continue to study the Book of Daniel. Hang in there! This is a cliff-hanger!

3

A FiERY FURNACE

63

Wasn't it exciting to watch God answer Daniel's prayer and give a very proud and self-willed king a glimpse into the future? You got a glimpse, too, and discovered that Jesus will not return to set up His kingdom until there are ten kings ruling on the earth. Pretty cool, huh?

Are you ready to find out what happens next? Let's head back to the set and get started on our new episode.

DAY ONE

SCENE ONE: AN IMAGE OF GOLD

"Hey, Mr. Andy, that's an awesome statue! What's it made of?" Max asked as he and Molly looked over Mr. Andy's huge prop for the third episode. Sam ran around in circles barking and growling. "Calm down, Sam," Max laughed, "it's not real. Come on, boy. We need to go help the actors run their lines before Aunt Sherry is ready to film."

Grab those scripts, and don't forget to talk to God! Help the actors run their lines. Turn to page 142. Read Daniel 3:1-6 and mark the key words listed on the next page for these verses

55

Guided Instruction

WEEK 3

DAY ONE

Daniel's friends, Shadrach, Meshach, and Abed-nego find themselves in serious trouble. But God faithfully continues to meet their needs.

Ask God to be with you as you study His Word. Put yourself in the place of these boys. Ask God to keep you steady, trusting His care.

63 Turn to page 55 and read "A Fiery Furnace" and "Scene One: An Image of Gold."

Guided Instruction

64 Turn to page 142 and copy key word markings to your bookmark and above the title "Daniel 3."

God (draw a purple triangle and color it yellow)

Nebuchadnezzar (color it orange)

Image (color it yellow)

Worship (circle it in purple and color it blue)

Deliver (draw a blue bowl and color it red)

Furnace of blazing fire (seven times more than it was usually heated, midst of the fire) (draw red fire around it)

Where (double-underline each word that denotes place)

When (draw a green clock over words that denote time)

65 Read Daniel 3:1-6 aloud using your Observation Worksheet visual aid as students follow along and call out each key word. Then mark them together as we noted on page 37.

---

on your Observation Worksheets. Then add any new words to your key-word bookmark.

Key-Word List for Daniel 3

God (draw a purple triangle and color it yellow)

64 Nebuchadnezzar (color it orange)

image (color it yellow)

worship (circle it in purple and color it blue)

deliver (draw a blue ⌣ and color it red)

furnace of blazing fire (seven times more than it was usually heated, midst of the fire) (draw red fire around it)

Don't forget to mark your pronouns! And mark anything that tells you WHERE by double-underlining the WHERE in green. Mark anything that tells you WHEN by drawing a green clock 🕐 or green circle like this: ◯.

(page 142)

the province of Babylon, while Daniel was at the king's court.

Chapter 3

65 1 Nebuchadnezzar the king made an image of gold, the height of which was sixty cubits and its width six cubits; he set it up on the plain of Dura in the province of Babylon.

2 Then Nebuchadnezzar the king sent word to assemble the satraps, the prefects and the governors, the counselors, the treasurers, the judges, the magistrates and all the rulers

of the provinces to come to the dedication of the image that Nebuchadnezzar the king had set up.

3 Then the satraps, the prefects and the governors, the counselors, the treasurers, the judges, the magistrates and all the rulers of the provinces were assembled for the dedication of the image that Nebuchadnezzar the king had set up; and they stood before the image that Nebuchadnezzar had set up.

4 Then the herald loudly proclaimed: "To you the command is given, O peoples, nations and men of every language,

5 that at the moment you hear the sound of the horn, flute, lyre, trigon, psaltery, bagpipe and all kinds of music, you are to fall down and worship the golden image that Nebuchadnezzar the king has set up.

6 "But whoever does not fall down and worship shall immediately be cast into the midst of a furnace of blazing fire."

7 Therefore, at that time, when all the peoples heard the sound

(page 56)

clock or green circle like this: ○.

Great work! Our scripts are marked and our actors are ready to go. Let's ask the 5 W's and an H so we can help Mr. Andy get set up for this opening scene.

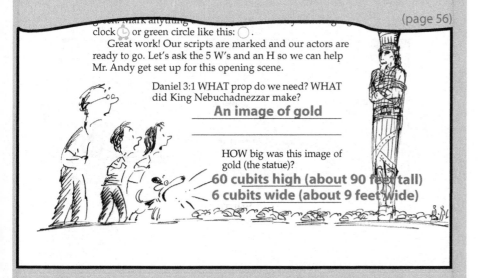

Daniel 3:1 WHAT prop do we need? WHAT did King Nebuchadnezzar make?

An image of gold

HOW big was this image of gold (the statue)?

60 cubits high (about 90 feet tall)
6 cubits wide (about 9 feet wide)

Guided Instruction

Read the selected verses to answer the questions.

Daniel 3:1 WHAT prop do we need? WHAT did King Nebuchadnezzar make? An image of gold

HOW big was this image of gold? 60 cubits high (about 90 feet tall); 6 cubits wide (about 9 feet wide)

Guided Instruction

Daniel 3:1 WHERE is our setting? WHERE did King Nebuchadnezzar set up this image of gold? <u>On the plain of</u> <u>Dura, south of Babylon</u>

66 Find the location on the map on page 57 and double-underline it green.

A Fiery Furnace   57

In our measurements, this would make the statue (the image of gold) 90 feet tall and 9 feet wide. Can you imagine a statue that tall? Why do you think that King Nebuchadnezzar built this huge image of gold? Could it be because of his dream?

A lot of Bible scholars believe that Nebuchadnezzar built this statue (the image of gold) in direct defiance of God. Remember, his dream meant that his great kingdom would end. He was only the head of gold, and there were three other kingdoms that would come after his. It's like he was saying to God, "Oh no, my kingdom isn't going to end! It's going to last forever!" King Nebuchadnezzar makes a mistake in thinking that he can change what's going to happen in the future, that he can change God's Word.

> Daniel 3:1 WHERE is our setting? WHERE did King Nebuchadnezzar set up this image of gold?
> **On the plain of Dura, south of Babylon**

Look at the map below. Find Babylon on your map. The city of Dura isn't shown on this map, but it would be about six miles south of Babylon.

NORTH

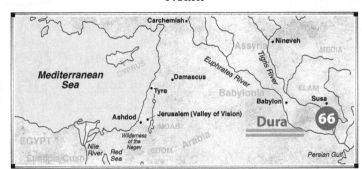

SOUTH

Daniel 3:2 To WHAT did King Nebuchadnezzar send word for all the satraps, prefects, governors, counselors, treasurers, judges, magistrates, and all the rulers of the provinces to come?

The ___dedication___ of the ___image___

Daniel 3:3-5 WHAT command was given to the people when they heard the music begin?

They were to ___fall___ ___down___ and ___worship___ the golden ___image___ that Nebuchadnezzar had set up.

Daniel 3:6 WHAT would happen if they didn't fall down and worship the image?

___They would be cast into a furnace of blazing fire.___

67 Why don't you fast-forward to the future just for a minute by looking up and reading Revelation 13:14-17 in your Bible.

Revelation 13:14 TO WHOM was there to be an image?

The beast

Revelation 13:15 WHAT would happen to those who did not worship the image of the beast?

They would be killed.

68 Can you believe that one day in the future there will be another image that those who dwell on the earth will have to worship or be killed? You can learn more about this beast, his image, and the future in Max and Molly's Revelation adventure, *A Sneak Peek into the Future.*

WHAT will happen on the plain of Dura? Will anyone refuse to bow down and worship Nebuchadnezzar's image of gold? We'll find out. But before we head out today, let's discover our new memory verse.

Guided Instruction

Daniel 3:2 To WHAT did King Nebuchadnezzar send word for all satraps, prefects, governors, counselors, treasurers, judges, magistrates, and all the rulers of the provinces to come? The dedication of the image

Daniel 3:3-5 WHAT command was given to the people when they heard the music begin? They were to fall down and worship the golden image that Nebuchadnezzar had set up.

Daniel 3:6 WHAT would happen if they didn't fall down and worship the image? They would be cast into a furnace of blazing fire.

67 Look up and read Revelation 13:14-17 to answer the next two questions.

Revelation 13:14 To WHOM was there to be an image? The beast

Revelation 13:15 WHAT would happen to those who did not worship the image of the beast? They would be killed.

68 Read the rest of the text on page 58-59 and elicit a discussion.

Guided Instruction

69 Look at the board on page 59. Cross out all words that make sounds. Place the remaining words in order on the blanks underneath.

"**But even if He does not,**

let it be known to you,

O King, that we are not

going to serve your gods or

worship the golden image that

you have set up."

Daniel 3:18

This is your memory verse. Copy it to an index card and read it three times, three times daily.

A Fiery Furnace   *59*

Look at the sound engineer's mixing board below. To discover this week's verse, look at the words written on the sound engineer's board. Put an X through each word on the board if it is a sound.

After you have crossed out all the sounds, take the words that are left on the board, starting with the words in the left handed column and then working through each column and placing them in order on the blanks underneath. Don't forget to find the reference for this verse in Daniel, chapter 3.

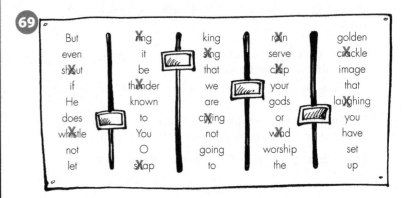

" <u>But</u>   <u>even</u>   <u>if</u>   <u>He</u>   <u>does</u>   <u>not</u> ,
<u>let</u>   <u>it</u>   <u>be</u>   <u>known</u>   <u>to</u>   <u>you</u> ,
<u>O</u>   <u>King</u> , <u>that</u>   <u>we</u>   <u>are</u>   <u>not</u>
<u>going</u>   <u>to</u>   <u>serve</u>   <u>your</u>   <u>gods</u>   <u>or</u>
<u>worship</u>   <u>the</u>   <u>golden</u>   <u>image</u>   <u>that</u>
<u>you</u>   <u>have</u>   <u>set</u>   <u>up</u> ."

Daniel 3:<u>18</u>

All right! Now practice saying your memory verse three times in a row, three times today!

SCENE TWO: SOUND THE MUSIC

(70) Hey, guys, welcome back to the set. Are you ready to find out what happens when the music sounds on the plain of Dura? All right! Why don't you help Mr. Morgan, the sound engineer? A sound engineer manages an audio crew that handles all the sounds on a television show. He or she uses monitors to help see what the camera sees, and a mixing board to balance all the sounds. A sound engineer needs to be fast-thinking and able to adapt to anything.

First talk to God. Then mark your script so that you will be ready to help Mr. Morgan. Be part of the audio crew and cue the musicians. Turn to page 143. Read Daniel 3:7-13 and mark the key words listed on page 56 for these verses on your Observation Worksheets or use your key-word bookmark.

Don't forget to mark the pronouns! And mark anything that tells you WHERE by double-underlining the WHERE in green. Mark anything that tells you WHEN by drawing a green clock or green circle like this: ◯.

(page 143)

(71) 7 Therefore at that time, when all the peoples heard the sound of the horn, flute, lyre, trigon, psaltery, bagpipe and all kinds of music, all the peoples, nations and men of every language fell down and worshiped the golden image that Nebuchadnezzar the king had set up.

8 For this reason at that time certain Chaldeans came forward and brought charges against the Jews.

9 They responded and said to Nebuchadnezzar the king: " O king, live forever!

10 "You, O king, have made a decree that every man who hears the sound of the horn, flute, lyre, trigon, psaltery, and bagpipe

---

Guided Instruction

Ask God to lead you to understanding of His Word. Today you will see that it is not always easy to see God in every situation. But He is with you in all things.

(70) Turn to page 60 and read "Scene Two: Sound the Music."

Review key words on page 56.

God (draw a purple triangle and color it yellow)

Nebuchadnezzar (color it orange)

Image (color it yellow)

Worship (circle it in purple and color it blue)

Deliver (draw a blue bowl and color it red)

Furnace of blazing fire (seven times more than it was usually heated, midst of the fire) (draw red fire around it)

Where (double-underline each word that denotes place)

When (draw a green clock over words that denote time)

(71) Turn to page 143 and read Daniel 3:7-13 aloud using your Observation Worksheet visual aid as students follow along and call out each key word. Then mark them together as we noted on page 37.

Guided Instruction

Then reread the selected verses to answer the questions.

Daniel 3:7 WHO bowed down and worshiped the image when the music was played? All the <u>peoples</u>, <u>nations</u> and <u>men</u> of every <u>language</u>

Daniel 3:8 WHAT did certain Chaldeans come forward to do? <u>They brought charges against the Jews.</u>

Daniel 3:10 WHAT was the decree they reminded King Nebuchadnezzar of? <u>Every man must worship the image.</u>

Daniel 3:11 WHAT would happen if they didn't fall down and worship? <u>They would be cast into the furnace of blazing fire.</u>

Daniel 3:12 WHAT did the Chaldeans tell King Nebuchadnezzar about Shadrach, Meshach, and Abed-nego? <u>They have disregarded you. They do not serve your gods or worship the image.</u>

---

144   *Observation Worksheets*

and all kinds of music, is to fall down and worship the golden image.

11 "But whoever does not fall down and worship shall be cast into the midst of a furnace of blazing fire."

12 "There are certain Jews whom you have appointed over the administration of the province of Babylon, namely Shadrach, Meshach and Abed-nego. These men, O king, have disregarded you; they do not serve your gods or worship the golden image which you have set up."

13 Then Nebuchadnezzar in rage and anger gave orders to bring Shadrach, Meshach and Abed-nego; then these men were brought before the king.

14 Nebuchadnezzar responded and said to them, "Is it true,

---

or green circle like this. ⌒ .

Now watch those monitors. Ask the 5 W's and an H.   (page 60)

Daniel 3:7 WHO bowed down and worshiped the image when the sound of the horn, flute, lyre, trigon, psaltery, bagpipe, and all kinds of music were heard?

All the __peoples__ , __nations__ and __men__ of every __language__

Daniel 3:8 WHAT did certain Chaldeans come forward to do?

__They brought charges against the Jews.__

A Fiery Furnace   61

Daniel 3:10 WHAT was the decree they reminded King Nebuchadnezzar of?
__Every man must worship the image.__

Daniel 3:11 WHAT would happen if they didn't fall down and worship?
__They would be cast into the furnace of blazing fire.__

Daniel 3:12 WHAT did the Chaldeans tell King Nebuchadnezzar about Shadrach, Meshach, and Abed-nego?
__They have disregarded you. They do not serve your gods or worship the image.__

(page 61)

Daniel 3:13 HOW did Nebuchadnezzar react? WHAT emotion does he show in this scene?

Rage and anger

Daniel 3:13 WHAT orders does King Nebuchadnezzar give?

To bring Shadrach, Meshach, and Abed-nego before the king

Wow! Three of our awesome teenagers are in trouble. They have not bowed to worship the image, and some of the Chaldeans just can't wait to tell the king that the Jews he has appointed over the province of Babylon have disregarded his command.

62   WEEK THREE

 WHY didn't Shadrach, Meshach, and Abed-nego bow down and worship this image? Just wait—you'll find out as we continue to film this exciting episode.

By the way, are you wondering where Daniel is? Look back at Daniel 2:49 on page 142. WHERE is Daniel?

He is at the king's court.

Daniel is not with Shadrach, Meshach, and Abed-nego in Dura. He is in Babylon at the king's court.

Don't forget to practice your memory verse. This verse shows us just how brave our three teenagers are! Would you have the courage to say this if you knew it would cost you your life? Think about it, and we'll see you back on the set tomorrow.

DAY THREE

Guided Instruction

Daniel 3:13 HOW did Nebuchadnezzar react? WHAT emotion does he show in this scene? Rage and anger

Daniel 3:13 WHAT orders does King Nebuchadnezzar give? To bring Shadrach, Meshach, and Abed-nego before the king

72 ELICIT DICUSSION. WHY didn't Shadrach, Meshach, and Abed-nego bow down and worship the image?

Daniel 2:49 WHERE is Daniel? He is at the king's court.

Practice saying the memory verse three times with a friend.

These boys are in big trouble! What would you do if you were in the same same situation?

Guided Instruction

Ask God to help you trust him regardless of what may happen in life. Ask Him to give you courage to face difficult circumstances like this one.

73 Turn to page 62 and read "Scene Three: A Raging King."

Review key words on page 56.

God (draw a purple triangle and color it yellow)

Nebuchadnezzar (color it orange)

Image (color it yellow)

Worship (circle it in purple and color it blue)

Deliver (draw a blue bowl and color it red)

Furnace of blazing fire (seven times more than it was usually heated, midst of the fire) (draw red fire around it)

Where (double-underline each word that denotes place)

When (draw a green clock over words that denote time)

74 Turn to page 144 and read Daniel 3:14-18 aloud using your Observation Worksheet visual aid as students follow along and call out each key word. Then mark them together as we noted on page 37.

(page 62)

SCENE THREE: A RAGING KING

73 You did a great job helping Mr. Morgan, our sound engineer, yesterday. Today Aunt Sherry needs you to help our cameraman, Mr. Grayson, as he captures the anger and rage of a very proud king. Ask God for His direction, and then zoom in to find out what happens as our three teenagers are brought before the king.

Turn to page 144. Read Daniel 3:14-18 and mark your key words listed on page 56 for these verses on your Observation Worksheets or use your key-word bookmark.

Don't forget to mark your pronouns!

(page 144)

brought before the king.

74 14 Nebuchadnezzar responded and said to them, "Is it true, Shadrach, Meshach and Abed-nego, that you do not serve my gods or worship the golden image that I have set up?

15 "Now if you are ready, at the moment you hear the sound of the horn, flute, lyre, trigon, psaltery and bagpipe and all kinds of music, to fall down and worship the image that I have made, very well. But if you do not worship, you will immediately be cast into the midst of a furnace of blazing fire; and what god is there who can deliver you out of my hands?"

16 Shadrach, Meshach and Abed-nego replied to the king, "O Nebuchadnezzar, we do not need to give you an answer concerning this matter.

17 "If it be so, our God whom we serve is able to deliver us from the furnace of blazing fire; and He will deliver us out of your hand, O king.

Observation Worksheets   145

18 "But even if He does not, let it be known to you, O king, that we are not going to serve your gods or worship the golden image that you have set up."

19 Then Nebuchadnezzar was filled with wrath, and his facial

(page 62)

Don't forget to mark your pronouns!

Daniel 3:14 WHAT does Nebuchadnezzar ask Shadrach, Meshach, and Abed-nego?

"Is it true, that you do not <u>serve</u> <u>my</u> <u>gods</u> or <u>worship</u> the golden <u>image</u> that I have set up?"

A Fiery Furnace   63

Daniel 3:15 WHAT does King Nebuchnezzar tell Shadrach, Meshach, and Abed-nego will happen to them if they don't worship the image?

<u>**They will be cast into the furnace of blazing fire.**</u>

75 Daniel 3:16 HOW do Shadrach, Meshach, and Abed-nego answer the king?

<u>**"We do not need to give you an answer concerning this matter."**</u>

Isn't that awesome? Look at how brave these three guys are! The king could immediately put them to death. But they tell the king they don't need to give him an answer. Their actions have spoken their answer. They did not bow down. They were the only ones left standing when the music played. The king has his answer.

76 WHY would Shadrach, Meshach, and Abed-nego refuse to bow down to King Nebuchadnezzar's image? Do you know? Let's look up Exodus 20:1-6. God is giving Moses the Ten Commandments.

Exodus 20:3 WHAT is the first commandment?

<u>**You shall have no other gods.**</u>

Exodus 20:4 WHAT did God tell them they were not to make?

<u>**You shall not make an idol.**</u>

Exodus 20:5 WHAT did God tell them they were not to do?

<u>**You shall not worship or serve them.**</u>

WHY were they not to worship them? WHAT does God tell them about Himself?

"I am a <u>jealous</u> <u>God</u>."

Shadrach, Meshach, and Abed-nego knew God, they knew

Guided Instruction

Read the selected verses to answer the questions.

Daniel 3:14 WHAT does Nebuchadnezzar ask Shadrach, Meshach, and Abed-nego? "Is it true, that you do not <u>serve my gods</u> or <u>worship</u> the golden <u>image</u> that I have set up?"

Daniel 3:15 WHAT does King Nebuchadnezzar tell Shadrach, Meshach, and Abed-Nego will happen to them if they don't worship the image? <u>They will be cast into the furnace of blazing fire.</u>

Daniel 3:16 HOW do Shadrach, Meshach, and Abed-nego answer the king? <u>"We do not need to give you an answer concerning this matter."</u>

75 ELICIT DISCUSSION about this event. Then look up the selected verses in Exodus.

Exodus 20:3 WHAT is the first commandment? <u>You shall have no other gods.</u>

Exodus 20:4 WHAT did God tell them they were not to make? <u>You shall not make an idol.</u>

Exodus 20:5 WHAT did God tell them they were not to do? <u>You shall not worship or serve them.</u>

WHY were they not to worship them? WHAT does God tell them about Himself? "I am a <u>jealous God</u>."

76 ELICIT DISCUSSION about these commandments.

Guided Instruction

Daniel 3:17 WHAT did they tell Nebuchadnezzar about God? *"Our God whom we* <u>serve</u> *is* <u>able</u> *to* <u>deliver</u> *us."*

Daniel 3:18 WHAT else do they tell the king? *"But even if He* <u>does not, let</u> *it be* <u>known</u> *to you, O King, that we are* <u>not</u> *going to* <u>serve</u> *your* <u>gods</u> *or* <u>worship</u> *the golden* <u>image</u> *that you set up."*

77 Read the rest of the text on pages 64-65 and lead a discussion about this story. Look up James 1:2-4 and read it to the students.

"Consider it all joy, my brethren, when you encounter various trials, knowing that the testing of your faith produces endurance. And let endurance have its perfect result, so that you may be perfect and complete, lacking in nothing."

James 1:2-4

---

64   WEEK THREE

His commandments, and they loved and worshiped the one and only true God!

Turn back to Daniel 3 on page 144.

Daniel 3:17 WHAT did they tell Nebuchadnezzar about God?

"Our God whom we ____serve____ is ____able____ to ____deliver____ us."

Daniel 3:18 WHAT else do they tell the king?

"But even if He ____does____ ____not____, ____let____ it be ____known____ to you, O king, that we are ____not____ going to ____serve____ your ____gods____ or ____worship____ the golden ____image____ that you have set up."

77 Wow! Just look at Shadrach, Meshach, and Abed-nego's faith and courage. Look at what they say: "Our God is able to deliver us." They know that God has the power to deliver them from the blazing fire, and that He will deliver them out of the king's hand.

But they also say, "Even if He does not…" Why do Shadrach, Meshach, and Abed-nego say this if they know God is able to deliver them? They know that God has the power to deliver, but they also know that God may choose not to. Sometimes God puts us in a fiery furnace to test our faith, to purify us, to make us more like Jesus (James 1:2-4).

God is able to deliver us from hard times, from sickness, and from death, but sometimes God chooses to let us go through these things to fulfill His purpose for our lives and to make us more like Jesus. Have you ever known someone who had cancer but was healed? How about someone else who had cancer and died? Sometimes God delivers us from the fire, sometimes He brings us through the fire, and then sometimes He delivers us into heaven. God is God, and He chooses the outcome.

Shadrach, Meshach, and Abed-nego trust God, even if it means they will go into the blazing fire, even if they die. They choose whom they will worship. They counted the cost of belonging to God. They chose to serve Him no matter the cost.

Look at their words: "Let it be known." They are saying "This is what we believe. These are our convictions. We have made up our minds. We will not change our beliefs. We will not conform. We will not do what everybody else is doing. We will not bend the knee. We will do what God says is right."

When we ask Jesus into our lives to be our Savior, He gets all of us. We totally belong to Him and not to ourselves anymore. We tell God, "You can do with me as You please." There will be kids who will want you to talk like them, listen to the music they listen to, and wear the same kinds of clothes that they wear. They will pressure you to be like them instead of like Jesus.

78 WHAT will you do? Have you made up your mind? Will you "let it be known"? Or will you bend the knee and be like everyone else? Take some time and think about what you believe, what your standards are. For example, will you listen to music that has bad words? Will you talk like everyone else, even if the words don't please God? Will you dress to be cool and popular, even if the clothing reveals too much or has a bad saying on it?

Write out your standards:

_____
_____
_____
_____
_____
_____
_____

Ask yourself, "Am I willing to live my life to please Jesus, not other people? Even if I am made fun of, called names, left out, or even have to die for what I believe, I will not bend. I will not bow. I will count the cost and follow Jesus." Be like

Shadrach, Meshach, and Abed-nego. Count the cost and decide that your life belongs to Jesus!

Way to go! What an awesome and intense scene. WHAT will happen when we film the next scene in this exciting episode? HOW will King Nebuchadnezzar react to Shadrach, Meshach, and Abed-nego's stand not to serve his gods or worship the golden image? You'll see! Now don't forget to practice your memory verse.

Guided Instruction

78 WHAT will YOU do? Let students have a few silent minutes to consider this question. Then tell them to write out their own standards.

Thank God that He is with you through all things.

Practice saying the memory verse three times with a friend. Can you say all of it without looking?

Guided Instruction

DAY FOUR

Ask God to enlighten you today, so that you will fully understand His Word.

79 Turn to page 66 and read "Scene Four: A Blazing Furnace."

Review key words on page 56.

God (draw a purple triangle and color it yellow)

Nebuchadnezzar (color it orange)

Image (color it yellow)

Worship (circle it in purple and color it blue)

Deliver (draw a blue bowl and color it red)

Furnace of blazing fire (seven times more than it was usually heated, midst of the fire) (draw red fire around it)

Where (double-underline each word that denotes place)

When (draw a green clock over words that denote time)

(page 66)

DAY FOUR

79 ## SCENE FOUR: A BLAZING FURNACE

"Wow," Max exclaimed as he looked around the set. "What is going on, Aunt Sherry?"

Aunt Sherry smiled as she pointed out the art director and stunt coordinator who were planning the next scene using special effects. "They are getting ready for us to shoot our next scene. It's going to be so cool. You get to watch them use a blue screen to film our characters. When a blue screen is used, only the characters are photographed by the camera. Then later the characters will be inserted into our scene of the fiery furnace using the computer to make it look like they are really there. You won't believe how awesome it is until you see it."

"That sounds amazing," Molly replied.

"Why don't you grab your scripts and finish marking them while we get ready to film?"

"That's a great idea, Aunt Sherry," said Max. "I'll pray, Molly, and then we can get to work."

All right! Now turn to page 145. Yesterday we left Shadrach, Meshach, and Abed-nego as they "let it be known" to

---

A Fiery Furnace   67

Nebuchadnezzar that they would not bow to, serve, or worship his gods and the image he had set up.

Read Daniel 3:19-26 and mark the key words listed on page 56 in these verses or use your key-word bookmark. Don't forget to mark your pronouns!

Now let's get ready to film this exciting scene. We're ready to roll. Play back music. Stand by... Ask those 5 W's and an H and direct King Nebuchadnezzar.

(page 145)

80 19 Then Nebuchadnezzar was filled with wrath, and his facial expression was altered toward Shadrach, Meshach and Abed-nego. He answered by giving orders to heat the furnace seven times more than it was usually heated.

20 He commanded certain valiant warriors who were in his army to tie up Shadrach, Meshach and Abed-nego in order to cast them into the furnace of blazing fire.

21 Then these men were tied up in their trousers, their coats, their caps and their other clothes, and were cast into the midst of the furnace of blazing fire.

22 For this reason, because the king's command was urgent and the furnace had been made extremely hot, the flame of the fire slew those men who carried up Shadrach, Meshach and Abed-nego.

23 But these three men, Shadrach, Meshach and Abed-nego, fell into the midst of the furnace of blazing fire still tied up.

24 Then Nebuchadnezzar the king was astounded and stood up in haste; he said to his high officials, "Was it not three men we cast bound into the midst of the fire?" They replied to the king, "Certainly, O king."

25 He said, "Look! I see four men loosed and walking about in the midst of the fire without harm, and the appearance of the fourth is like a son of the gods!"

26 Then Nebuchadnezzar came near to the door of the furnace

146   *Observation Worksheets*

of blazing fire; he responded and said, "Shadrach, Meshach and Abed-nego, come out, you servants of the Most High God, and come here!" Then Shadrach, Meshach and Abed-nego came out of the midst of the fire.

27 The satraps, the prefects, the governors and the king's high

Guided Instruction

80 Turn to page 145 and read Daniel 3:19-26 aloud using your Observation Worksheet visual aid as students follow along and call out each key word. Then mark them together as we noted on page 37.

Guided Instruction

Read the selected verses to answer the questions.

Daniel 3:19 HOW does Nebuchadnezzar react to Shadrach, Meshach, and Abed-nego? He's filled with <u>wrath</u>.

WHAT are his lines? He gave orders to <u>heat the furnace seven times hotter than usual</u>.

Daniel 3:20 WHAT were his commands? <u>He commanded warriors to tie up Shadrach, Meshach, and Abed-nego and cast them into the furnace of blazing fire.</u>

Daniel 3:21-22 WHAT happened to the men who carried up Shadrach, Meshach, and Abed-nego and threw them into the furnace? <u>The flames from the furnace killed them.</u>

(81) Draw a picture of this scene in the box on page 68.

Daniel 3:23 WHAT do we see about Shadrach, Meshach, and Abed-nego as they are thrown into the fire? <u>They are in the midst of the fire, still tied up.</u>

(page 67)

...ect King Nebuchadnezzar.

Daniel 3:19 HOW does Nebuchadnezzar react to Shadrach, Meshach, and Abed-nego's answer?

He was filled with ____<u>wrath</u>____ .

WHAT are his lines?

He gave orders to <u>heat the furnace seven times hotter than usual</u> .

Wow! Look at how angry the king is. He wants the furnace heated seven times more than it was usually heated.

Daniel 3:20 WHAT were his commands?

<u>He commanded warriors to tie up Shadrach, Meshach, and Abed-nego. and cast them into the furnace of blazing fire.</u>

Daniel 3:21-22 WHAT happened to the men who carried up Shadrach, Meshach, and Abed-nego and threw them in?

<u>The flames from the furnace killed them.</u>

_____

_____

_____

---

68   WEEK THREE

Draw a picture in the box below to show this amazing scene.

(81)

Daniel 3:23 WHAT do we see about Shadrach, Meshach, and Abed-nego as they are thrown into the fire?

<u>They are in the midst of the fire, still tied up.</u>

Daniel 3:24-25 WHAT does Nebuchadnezzar see?

(page 68)

Daniel 3:24-25 WHAT does Nebuchadnezzar see?

HOW many were thrown in?
Three

HOW many were in the furnace?
Four

HOW does Nebuchadnezzar describe this fourth one?
"The fourth one appeared like a son of the gods."

WHO was the fourth? Do you have any idea?
Some think Jesus Christ.

Do you know who this fourth one is that Nebuchadnezzar says looks like "a son of the gods"? Most Bible scholars think

---

A Fiery Furnace   69

that this is Jesus before He left heaven and came to earth as a baby in the New Testament. Sometimes in the Old Testament before Jesus was born, He would make appearances on Earth.

Draw a picture of Daniel 3:24-25 in the box to show what this exciting scene will look like on film.

Guided Instruction

Daniel 3:24-25 WHAT does Nebuchadnezzar see? HOW many were thrown in? <u>Three</u>

HOW many were in the furnace? <u>Four</u>

HOW does Nebuchadnezzar describe this fourth one? <u>"The fourth one appeared like a son of the gods."</u>

WHO was the fourth man? Do you have any idea? <u>Some think Jesus Christ.</u>

82 Draw a picture of this scene in the box on page 69.

Guided Instruction

Daniel 3:26 WHAT does Nebuchadnezzar say to Shadrach, Meshach, and Abed-nego? "Servants of the Most High God, come out."

WOW! Isn't our God awesome? Aren't you excited about God's faithfulness and compassion?

You have diligently worked through these Scriptures. God is pleased.

(page 69)

Daniel 3:26 WHAT does Nebuchadnezzar say to Shadrach, Meshach, and Abed-nego?

"Servants of the Most High God, come out."

Are you *amazed* that Jesus was with our three awesome teenagers in the midst of the fire? Remember, when we invite Jesus into our lives, Jesus comes to live in us (John 14:23). Jesus will be with us no matter what we go through.

What will Shadrach, Meshach, and Abed-nego look like when they come out of the furnace, since we saw the valiant warriors who threw them in burned up? Will there be any marks or burns on them? Will they smell like smoke? We'll find out.

70   WEEK THREE

(83) SCENE FIVE: SERVANTS OF GOD MOST HIGH

WHAT an awesome scene! We can't wait to see this episode once Miss Lenyer, our digital artist, has added in all those cool special effects. Today we need to film our final scene in this episode. Pray and then pull out your scripts.

Turn to page 146. Read Daniel 3:27-30 and mark the key words listed on page 56 in these verses or use your key-word bookmark.

Don't forget to mark your pronouns! And mark anything that tells you WHERE by double-underlining the WHERE in green.

Now help Mr. Jackson with the makeup to show what our

(page 146)

of the midst of the fire.

84 27 The satraps, the prefects, the governors and the king's high officials gathered around and saw in regard to these men that the fire had no effect on the bodies of these men nor was the hair of their head singed, nor were their trousers damaged, nor had the smell of fire even come upon them.

28 Nebuchadnezzar responded and said, "Blessed be the God of Shadrach, Meshach and Abed-nego, who has sent His angel and delivered His servants who put their trust in Him, violating the king's command, and yielded up their bodies so as not to serve or worship any god except their own God.

29 "Therefore I make a decree that any people, nation or tongue that speaks anything offensive against the God of Shadrach, Meshach and Abed-nego shall be torn limb from limb and their houses reduced to a rubbish heap, inasmuch as there is no other god who is able to deliver in this way."

30 Then the king caused Shadrach, Meshach and Abed-nego to prosper in the province of Babylon.

Guided Instruction

Thank God that He cares about you and about everything in your life. Ask Him to be with you as you complete this study of His Word.

83 Turn to page 70 and read "Scene Five: Servants of God Most High."

Review key words on page 56.

God (draw a purple triangle and color it yellow)

Nebuchadnezzar (color it orange)

Image (color it yellow)

Worship (circle it in purple and color it blue)

Deliver (draw a blue bowl and color it red)

Furnace of blazing fire (seven times more than it was usually heated, midst of the fire) (draw red fire around it)

Where (double-underline in green each word that denotes place)

When (draw a green clock over words that denote time)

84 Turn to page 146 and read Daniel 3:27-30 aloud using your Observation Worksheet visual aid as students follow along and call out each key word. Then mark them together as we noted on page 37.

Guided Instruction

Read the selected verses to answer the questions.

Daniel 3:27 WHAT did the king's high officials see about Shadrach, Meshach, and Abed-nego? The fire had no effect on their bodies, hair, or clothes. There was no smell of fire on them.

Daniel 3:28 HOW does Nebuchadnezzar react? WHAT does he say? "Blessed be the God of Shadrach, Meshach, and Abed-nego."

WHOM did Nebuchadnezzar say God sent to deliver His servants? His angel

Daniel 3:28 WHY were they delivered? Because they put their trust in God

WHAT did Shadrach, Meshach, and Abed-nego do? They y i e l d e d up their bodies so as not to serve or worship any god except their own God.

Daniel 3:29 WHAT is Nebuchadnezzar's decree? No one is to speak against the God of Shadrach, Meshach, and Abed-nego.

WHAT will happen if they speak against God? They will be torn limb from limb and their houses will be reduced to a rubbish heap.

WHAT does Nebuchadnezzar say about God? There is no other god who can deliver.

Daniel 3:30 WHAT happened to Shadrach, Meshach, and Abed-nego? The king caused them to prosper.

(page 70)

three teenagers look like as they come out of the fire. Ask those 5 W's and an H.

Daniel 3:27 WHAT did the king's high officials see about Shadrach, Meshach, and Abed-nego?

The fire had no effect on their bodies, hair, or clothes.

There was no smell of fire on them.

Isn't that cool? Here they are in the middle of the fire, and there is no effect of the fire on them: no burns, no singed hair, no smell of the fire. God is so *awesome!*

Daniel 3:28 HOW does Nebuchadnezzar react? WHAT does he say?

" Blessed be the God of Shadrach , Meshach , and Abed-nego ."

WHOM did Nebuchadnezzar say God sent to deliver His servants?

His angel

A Fiery Furnace   71

Daniel 3:28 WHY were they delivered?

Because they put their trust in God

WHAT did Shadrach, Meshach, and Abed-nego do?

They y i e l d e d up their bodies so as not to serve or worship any god except their own God .

Look at our brave teenagers' witness to a proud king! They are willing to go against the king, to give up their lives in order to not worship anyone but the one true God! Incredible!

Daniel 3:29 WHAT is Nebuchadnezzar's decree?

No one is to speak against the God of Shadrach, Meshach, and Abed-nego.

WHAT will happen if they speak anything offensive against God?

They will be torn limb from limb and their houses will be reduced to a rubbish heap.

WHAT does Nebuchadnezzar say about God?

There is no other god who can deliver.

Wow! Nebuchadnezzar recognizes there is no other god like God!

Daniel 3:30 WHAT happened to Shadrach, Meshach, and Abed-nego?

The king caused them to prosper.

through

(page 71)

85 Look at how God honored their faith. When you go through the fire and God purifies you to be more like Jesus, then He can use you in ways you never dreamed possible. On the lines below, write a prayer to God and ask Him to work in your life so He can use you:

86
_____
_____
_____

---

72   WEEK THREE
_____

Cut and print! That was good! Way to go! We can't wait to see this exciting episode. You have done an awesome job this week! Don't forget to say your memory verse to a grown-up. Ask that person what he or she is willing to "let it be known" about him or her. See you back on the set next week.

Guided Instruction

85 ELICIT DISCUSSION about how God honored their faith.

86 Write a prayer to God and ask Him to use you to build His kingdom.

If you are a classroom teacher you may want to give your students a quiz on their memory verse. There is also a quiz on Week Three on page 155 to check memory and understanding.

A great game to play with your kids to review all they have learned is the *Drawing Game* on page 162.

Guided Instruction

WEEK 4

DAY ONE

Sometimes God does something drastic to get a man's attention. King Nebuchadnezzar was an arrogant man, trusting in his own power. God used some scary experiences to show this king that He's Lord of lords.

Ask God to make you keep your eyes on Him alone. He is with you all the time. Ask Him to give you understanding of His message today.

87 Turn to page 73 and read "Daniel 4" and "Scene One: Nebuchadnezzar's Palace."

4

A VISION OF A STRONG TREE

DANIEL 4

Wow! Were you shocked last week when you saw King Nebuchadnezzar create a golden image and decide that everyone must worship it or die? Three brave young men let it be known they would not bend their knees so they ended up in a fiery furnace and were delivered by God. WHAT a suspenseful episode! WHAT will happen next? Grab those scripts and let's find out.

DAY ONE

87 **SCENE ONE: NEBUCHADNEZZAR'S PALACE**

"Wow, Aunt Sherry, those special effects are so cool!" Molly exclaimed as she, Max, and Aunt Sherry finished watching the completed episode on the fiery furnace.

"It sure was!" Max joined in. "I can't get over how incredible those scenes are of the men being incinerated into ashes as they throw Shadrach, Meshach, and Abed-nego into the fiery furnace."

"It's pretty amazing what you can do with special effects,"

73

Aunt Sherry replied. "Are you ready to head back to the set and mark those scripts?"

"We sure are," Max replied. "Let's go, Molly."

Now that we are back on the set, don't forget to pray. Then turn to page 146. Read Daniel 4:1-9 and mark the key words listed below on your Observation Worksheets. Add any new key words to your key-word bookmark.

Key-Word List for Daniel 4

88

God (Most High, King of heaven) (draw a purple triangle and color it yellow)

Daniel (Belteshazzar) (color it blue)

dream (vision) (draw a blue cloud around it)

Nebuchadnezzar (color it orange)

kingdom (draw a purple crown and color it blue)

sin (iniquities) (color it brown)

Don't forget to mark your pronouns! And mark anything that tells WHEN by drawing a green clock 🕐 or green circle like this: ◯.

All right! Now that our scripts are marked, let's find out ~~prosper in the province of Babylon.~~

Chapter 4

89 1 Nebuchadnezzar the king to all the peoples, nations, and men of every language that live in all the earth: "May your peace abound!

Observation Worksheets   147

2 "It has seemed good to me to declare the signs and wonders which the Most High God has done for me.

3 "How great are His signs

And how mighty are His wonders!

His kingdom is an everlasting kingdom

And His dominion is from generation to generation.

4 ~~"I, N~~ishing in

Guided Instruction

88 Turn to page 146 and copy the key word markings found on page 74 above the Daniel 4 title and to your bookmark.

God (Most High, King of heaven) (draw a purple triangle and color it yellow)

Daniel (Belteshazzar) (color it blue)

Dream (vision) (draw a blue cloud around it)

Nebuchadnezzar (color it orange)

Kingdom (draw a purple crown and color it blue)

Sin (iniquities) (color it brown)

Where (double-underline words that denote place in green)

When (draw a green clock over words that denote time)

89 Read Daniel 4:1-9 aloud using your Observation Worksheet visual aid as students follow along and call out each key word. Then mark them together as we noted on page 37.

Guided Instruction

Read the selected verses to answer the questions.

Daniel 4:1-4 WHO is writing this chapter? WHO is speaking? <u>King Nebuchadnezzar is speaking to all the peoples, nations, and men of every language that live in all the earth.</u>

(page 147)

4 "I, Nebuchadnezzar, was at ease in my house and flourishing in my palace.

5 "I saw a dream and it made me fearful; and these fantasies as I lay on my bed and the visions in my mind kept alarming me.

6 "So I gave orders to bring into my presence all the wise men of Babylon, that they might make known to me the interpretation of the dream.

7 "Then the magicians, the conjurers, the Chaldeans and the diviners came in and I related the dream to them, but they could not make its interpretation known to me.

8 "But finally Daniel came in before me, whose name is Belteshazzar according to the name of my god, and in whom is a spirit of the holy gods; and I related the dream to him, saying,

9 'O Belteshazzar, chief of the magicians, since I know that a spirit of the holy gods is in you and no mystery baffles you, tell me the visions of my dream which I have seen, along with its interpretation.

10 'Now the visions in my mind as I lay on my bed:

(page 74)

like this: ◯ .

All right! Now that our scripts are marked, let's find out what is happening in chapter 4. Ask those 5 W's and an H.

Daniel 4:1-4 WHO is writing this chapter? WHO is speaking?

<u>King Nebuchadnezzar is speaking to all the peoples, nations, and men of every language that live in all the earth.</u>

Daniel 4:2 WHAT is King Nebuchadnezzar doing?
Declaring the signs and wonders of the Most High God

Are you surprised to see King Nebuchadnezzar declaring these things about God? Make a list in the box below to show what you learned about God in verses 2-3.

What I Learned About God

(90)

Daniel 4:2 He is God most high.

He has done signs and wonders.

Daniel 4:3 His signs are great.

His wonders are mighty.

His kingdom is an everlasting kingdom.

His dominion is from generation to generation.

Daniel 4:4 WHERE is Nebuchadnezzar?
In his palace

Daniel 4:5 WHAT does Nebuchadnezzar see?
A dream

HOW does Nebuchadnezzar react to this vision?
He's afraid; they alarmed him.

Daniel 4:6 WHOM does Nebuchadnezzar bring into his presence?
All the wise men of Babylon

Guided Instruction

Daniel 4:2 WHAT is King Nebuchadnezzar doing? <u>Declaring the signs and wonders of the Most High God</u>

(90) In the box on page 75, list what you learned about God in verses 2-3.

What I learned about God

Daniel 4:2 <u>He is God most high.</u>

<u>He has done signs and wonders.</u>

Daniel 4:3 <u>His signs are great.</u>

<u>His wonders are mighty.</u>

<u>His kingdom is an everlasting kingdom.</u>

<u>His dominion is from generation to generation.</u>

Daniel 4:4 WHERE is Nebuchadnezzar? <u>In his palace</u>

Daniel 4:5 WHAT does Nebuchadnezzar see? <u>A dream</u>

HOW does Nebuchadnezzar react to these visions? <u>He's afraid; they alarmed him.</u>

Daniel 4:6 WHOM does Nebuchadnezzar bring into his presence? <u>All the wise men of Babylon</u>

Guided Instruction

WHY does he send for them? <u>To interpret his dream</u>

Daniel 4:7 Can they tell Nebuchadnezzar what the dream means? <u>No.</u>

Daniel 4:8 WHOM does Nebuchadnezzar send for next? <u>Daniel</u>

Daniel 4:9 WHAT does Nebuchadnezzar say about Daniel? "O Belteshazzar, <u>chief</u> of the <u>magicians</u>...a <u>spirit</u> of the <u>holy gods</u> is in you and no <u>mystery</u> baffles you."

---

76   WEEK FOUR

WHY does he send for them?
To interpret his dream

Daniel 4:7 Can they tell Nebuchadnezzar what the dream means?
No.

Daniel 4:8 WHOM does Nebuchadnezzar send for next?
Daniel

Daniel 4:9 WHAT does Nebuchadnezzar say about Daniel?

"O Belteshazzar, __**chief**__ of the __**magicians**__ ... a __**spirit**__ of the __**holy**__ __**gods**__ is in you and no __**mystery**__ baffles you."

Isn't it fantastic the way Nebuchadnezzar sees that Daniel has a different spirit in him? Will Daniel (Belteshazzar) be able to tell the king his dream? We'll find out as we finish this scene tomorrow. But before we leave the set, we need to discover our new memory verse.

Look at the three rolls of film on the next page. One of these three rolls gives you the correct words for your memory verse this week. To find the correct roll of film, look through Daniel 4 on pages 146-151 and at the book on page 77.

Find which roll of film's words fit the blanks on the script. Then circle that roll of film and fill in the blanks with the correct words to complete your verse. Don't forget to write down the reference. Practice this verse three times today!

Way to go! You did it!

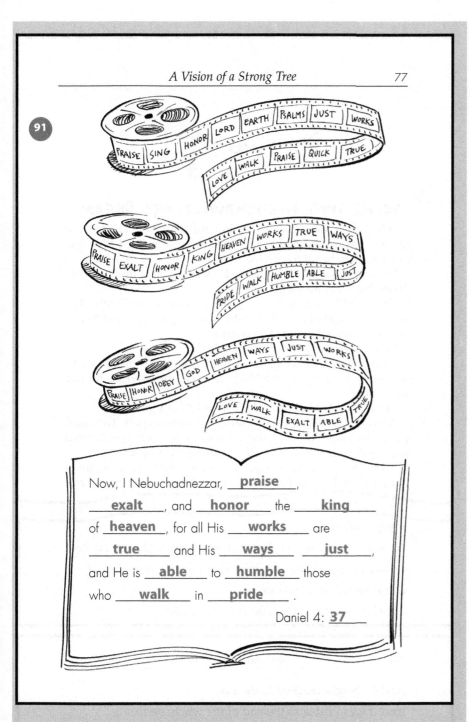

Now, I Nebuchadnezzar, **praise**, **exalt**, and **honor** the **king** of **heaven**, for all His **works** are **true** and His **ways** **just**, and He is **able** to **humble** those who **walk** in **pride**.

Daniel 4: **37**

Guided Instruction

91 Look at the three reels on page 77. Compare them to the verses in Daniel 4 and complete the blanks on the scroll. Then copy it to an index card. This is your Memory Verse.

"Now, I Nebuchadnezzar, <u>praise</u>, <u>exalt</u>, and <u>honor</u> the <u>king</u> of <u>heaven</u>, for all His <u>works</u> are <u>true</u> and His <u>ways</u> <u>just</u>, and He is <u>able</u> to <u>humble</u> those who <u>walk</u> in <u>pride</u>."

Daniel 4:<u>37</u>

Read your Memory Verse three times, three times each day.

Guided Instruction

Nebuchadnezzar started praising God in Daniel 4. But he gets full of himself and forgets who is in charge.

Ask God to keep you mindful of His sovereignty and to help you study His Word with understanding.

92 Turn to page 78 and read "Scene Two: Nebuchadnezzar's Dream."

Review key words on page 74.

God (Most High, King of heaven) (draw a purple triangle and color it yellow)

Daniel (Belteshazzar) (color it blue)

Dream (vision) (draw a blue cloud around it)

Nebuchadnezzar (color it orange)

Kingdom (draw a purple crown and color it blue)

Sin (iniquities) (color it brown)

Where (double-underline words that denote place in green)

When (draw a green clock over words that denote time)

93 Turn to page 147 and read Daniel 4:10-17 aloud using your Observation Worksheet visual aid as students follow along and call out each key word. Then mark them together as we noted on page 37.

92

SCENE TWO: NEBUCHADNEZZAR'S DREAM

"Hey, guys, are you ready to find out what Nebuchadnezzar dreams that has him so fearful?" Aunt Sherry asked Max and Molly as they headed onto the set.

"We can't wait!" Molly replied. "It must be some dream to alarm this arrogant king."

"Wait until we film it. It is going to look so cool with Miss Lenyer's special effects. But first I want to give you and Max a chance to create a set of storyboards."

"What are storyboards?" Max asked.

"Storyboards are sketches of the main scenes in our television show. I want you and Molly to create storyboards for our next scene."

"That sounds like fun," Max replied. "Let's go."

Now that we're back on the set, don't forget to pray. Then turn to page 147. Read Daniel 4:10-17 and mark your key words listed on page 74 in these verses or use your key-word bookmark.

Don't forget to mark your pronouns! And mark anything that tells WHEN by drawing a green clock 🕐 or green circle like this.

(page 147)

93 interpretation.

10 'Now these were the visions in my mind as I lay on my bed: I was looking, and behold, there was a tree in the midst of the earth and its height was great.

11 'The tree grew large and became strong

148　　　　*Observation Worksheets*

And its height reached to the sky,

And it was visible to the end of the whole earth.

12 'Its foliage was beautiful and its fruit abundant,

And in it was food for all.

The beasts of the field found shade under it,

And the birds of the sky dwelt in its branches,

And all living creatures fed themselves from it.

(page 148)

And all living creatures fed themselves from it.

13 'I was looking in the visions in my mind as I lay on my bed, and behold, an angelic watcher, a holy one, descended from heaven.

14 'He shouted out and spoke as follows:

" Chop down the tree and cut off its branches,

Strip off its foliage and scatter its fruit;

Let the beasts flee from under it

And the birds from its branches.

15 "Yet leave the stump with its roots in the ground,

But with a band of iron and bronze around it

In the new grass of the field;

And let him be drenched with the dew of heaven,

And let him share with the beasts in the grass

of the earth.

16 "Let his mind be changed from that of a man

And let a beast's mind be given to him,

And let seven periods of time pass over him.

17 "This sentence is by the decree of the angelic watchers

And the decision is a command of the holy ones,

In order that the living may know

(page 78)

...ens WHEN by drawing a green clock or g... like this: ◯ .

Daniel 4:10 WHAT was Nebuchadnezzar's vision?
A tree in the midst of the earth

Daniel 4:11 WHAT do we see about this tree?
It grew large and became strong.

Daniel 4:12 WHAT do we see about the tree's foliage?
It's beautiful.

_____

Guided Instruction

Read the selected verses to answer the questions.

Daniel 4:10 WHAT was Nebuchadnezzar's vision? A tree in the midst of the earth

Daniel 4:11 WHAT do we see about this tree? It grew large and became strong.

Daniel 4:12 WHAT do we see about the tree's foliage? It's beautiful.

Guided Instruction

WHAT does the tree provide for the beasts, birds, and living creatures?
Fruit for food, shade, and branches to nest in

94 Draw a sketch from Daniel 4:10-12 for the storyboard scene in the box on page 79.

Daniel 4:13 WHAT does Daniel see descend from heaven? An angelic watcher

Daniel 4:14 WHAT does this angelic watcher shout out? "Chop down the tree and cut off its branches, strip off its foliage and scatter its fruit; let the beast flee from under it and the birds from its branches."

A Vision of a Strong Tree   79

WHAT does the tree provide for the beasts, birds, and living creatures?

Fruit for food, shade, and branches to nest in

Now create your first storyboard by sketching the scene in Daniel 4:10-12 in the box below.

Daniel 4:13 WHAT does Daniel see descend from heaven?

An angelic watcher

Daniel 4:14 WHAT does this angelic watcher shout out?

" Chop down the tree and cut off its branches , strip off its foliage and scatter its fruit ; let the beast flee from under it and the birds from its branches ."

80   WEEK FOUR

Draw this storyboard for Daniel 4:13-14 in the box below.

95

Daniel 4:15 WHAT else did the angelic watcher shout out?

"Leave the __stump__ with its __roots__ in the ground, but with a __band__ of __iron__ and __bronze__ around it… and let him be drenched with the __dew__ of __heaven__, and let him __share__ with the __beast__ in the __grass__ of the __earth__."

Daniel 4:16 "Let his __mind__ be __changed__ from that of a __man__ and let a __beast's__ __mind__ be given to him, and let __seven__ __periods__ of time pass over him."

Create your next storyboard by sketching Daniel 4:15-16 in the box on the next page.

Guided Instruction

95 Draw a sketch from Daniel 4:13-14 for the storyboard scene in the box on page 80.

Daniel 4:15 WHAT else did the angelic watcher shout out? "Leave the <u>stump</u> with its <u>roots</u> in the ground, but with a <u>band</u> of <u>iron</u> and <u>bronze</u> around it… and let him be drenched with the <u>dew</u> of <u>heaven</u> and let him <u>share</u> with the <u>beast's</u> in the <u>grass</u> of the <u>earth</u>."

Daniel 4:16 "Let his <u>mind</u> be <u>changed</u> from that of a <u>man</u> and let a <u>beast's</u> <u>mind</u> be given to him, and let <u>seven</u> <u>periods</u> of time pass over him."

Guided Instruction

96 Draw a sketch from Daniel 4:15-16 for the storyboard scene in the box on page 81.

Daniel 4:17 WHY does Nebuchadnezzar receive this dream? WHAT are the living to know? "That the Most High is ruler over the realm of mankind, and bestows it on whom He wishes and sets over it the lowest of men."

Practice saying the Memory Verse three times with a friend.

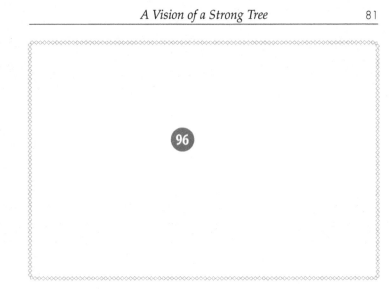

A Vision of a Strong Tree   81

96

Outstanding artwork! Now look at Daniel 4:17.

WHY does Nebuchadnezzar receive this dream? WHAT are the living to know?

"That the ___Most___ ___High___ is ___ruler___ over the realm of ___mankind___, and ___bestows___ it on whom He ___wishes___ and sets over it the ___lowest___ of ___men___."

WHAT does it mean that God is God Most High? The Hebrew name for God Most High is *El Elyon* (pronounced *el el-YON*). This is the name of God that shows us that God is the Possessor of heaven and earth. God is sovereign. *Sovereign* means that God is the Ruler over *everything!* There is absolutely nothing that God doesn't have control over! Amazing!

Are you curious about King Nebuchadnezzar's unusual dream? WHAT could this tree and it being chopped down mean?

Don't forget to practice your memory verse. See you on the set tomorrow!

DAY THREE

This is a scary story. But remember, God sometimes has to shake us up to get our attention.

Ask God to make reveal a special message from His Word today.

97 Turn to page 82 and read "Scene Three: Daniel Interprets the Dream."

Review key words on page 74.

God (Most High, King of heaven) (draw a purple triangle and color it yellow)

Daniel (Belteshazzar) (color it blue)

Dream (vision) (draw a blue cloud around it)

Nebuchadnezzar (color it orange)

Kingdom (draw a purple crown and color it blue)

Sin (iniquities) (color it brown)

Where (double-underline words that denote place in green)

When (draw a green clock over words that denote time)

98 Turn to page 149 and read Daniel 4:18-27 aloud using your Observation Worksheet visual aid as students follow along and call out each key word. Then mark them together as we noted on page 37.

---

82   WEEK FOUR

97

SCENE THREE: DANIEL INTERPRETS THE DREAM

It's great to have you back! Miss Anna, the production manager, needs your help to make sure everyone is where they're supposed to be. Why don't you get on the walkie-talkie and make sure King Nebuchadnezzar and Daniel are ready for our next scene?

Don't forget to pray. Then turn to page 149. Read Daniel 4:18-27 and mark the key words listed on page 74 in these verses or use your key-word bookmark.

Don't forget to mark your pronouns! And mark anything that tells WHEN by drawing a green clock 🕐 or green circle like this:◯.

(page 149)

And sets over it the lowliest of men."

98 18 'This is the dream which I, King Nebuchadnezzar, have seen. Now you, Belteshazzar, tell me its interpretation, inasmuch as none of the wise men of my kingdom is able to make known to me the interpretation; but you are able, for a spirit of the holy gods is in you.'

19 "Then Daniel, whose name is Belteshazzar, was appalled for a while as his thoughts alarmed him. The king responded and said, 'Belteshazzar, do not let the dream or its interpretation alarm you.' Belteshazzar replied, ' My lord, if only the dream applied to those who hate you and its interpretation to your adversaries!

20 'The tree that you saw, which became large and grew strong, whose height reached to the sky and was visible to all the earth

21 and whose foliage was beautiful and its fruit abundant, and in which was food for all, under which the beasts of the field dwelt and in whose branches the birds of the sky lodged—

22 it is you, O king; for you have become great and grown strong, and your majesty has become great and reached to the sky and your dominion to the end of the earth.

23 'In the king's dream an angelic watcher, a holy one, descend-

Guided Instruction

Read the selected verses to answer the questions.

Daniel 4:19 HOW did Daniel react to the king's dream? He was <u>appalled</u>; his thoughts <u>alarmed</u> him.

Daniel 4:20-22 WHOM does the tree represent in the dream? <u>King Nebuchadnezzar</u>

(page 149)

sky and your dominion to the end of the earth.

23 'In that the king saw an angelic watcher, a holy one, descending from heaven and saying, "Chop down the tree and destroy it; yet leave the stump with its roots in the ground, but with a band of iron and bronze around it in the new grass of the field, and let him be drenched with the dew of heaven, and let him

---

150   *Observation Worksheets*

share with the beasts of the field until seven periods of time pass over him,"

24 this is the interpretation, O king, and this is the decree of the Most High, which has come upon my lord the king:

25 that you be driven away from mankind and your dwelling place be with the beasts of the field, and you be given grass to eat like cattle and be drenched with the dew of heaven; and seven periods of time will pass over you, until you recognize that the Most High is ruler over the realm of mankind and bestows it on whomever He wishes.

26 'And in that it was commanded to leave the stump with the roots of the tree, your kingdom will be assured to you after you recognize that it is Heaven that rules.

27 'Therefore, O king, may my advice be pleasing to you: break away now from your sins by doing righteousness and from your iniquities by showing mercy to the poor, in case there may be a prolonging of your prosperity.'

---

like this: ○.

(page 82)

   Great work! Quiet on the set! Camera One, pick up on Daniel. Come in tight. We need a close-up as he responds to the king's dream.

Bring on Neb

Daniel 4:19 HOW did Daniel react to the king's dream?

He was _____<u>appalled</u>_____; his thoughts <u>alarmed</u> him.

Daniel 4:20-22 WHOM does the tree represent in the dream?
_____**King Nebuchadnezzar**_____

Daniel 4:22 WHAT does Daniel say this tree shows us about the king?

99 "You have become ___great___ and grown ___strong___, and your ___majesty___ has become great and reached to the sky and your ___dominion___ to the end of the ___earth___."

Daniel 4:23-25 WHAT is going to happen to Nebuchadnezzar? WHAT is the decree of the Most High to the king?

"That you be ___driven___ away from ___mankind___ and your ___dwelling___ place be with the ___beasts___ of the field, and you be given ___grass___ to ___eat___ like cattle and be drenched with the ___dew___ of ___heaven___; and ___seven___ ___periods___ of time will pass over you."

Guided Instruction

Daniel 4:22 WHAT does Daniel say the tree shows us about the king?
"You have become <u>great</u> and grown <u>strong</u> and your <u>majesty</u> has become great and reached to the sky and your <u>dominion</u> to the end of the <u>earth</u>."

99 ELICIT DISCUSION about this. King Nebuchadnezzar was getting too big for his own good.

Daniel 4:23-25 WHAT is going to happen to Nebuchadnezzar? WHAT is the decree of the Most High to the king? "That you be <u>driven</u> away from <u>mankind</u> and your <u>dwelling</u> place be with the <u>beasts</u> of the field, and you be given <u>grass</u> to <u>eat</u> like cattle and be drenched with the <u>dew</u> of <u>heaven</u>; and <u>seven</u> <u>periods</u> of time will pass over you."

Guided Instruction

Daniel 4:25 Until WHEN? WHAT is King Nebuchadnezzar to recognize? "That the <u>Most High</u> is <u>ruler</u> over the realm of <u>mankind</u> and <u>bestows</u> it on whomever He <u>wishes</u>."

Daniel 4:26 WHY is the stump with the roots of the tree left? To show Nebuchadnezzar that his <u>kingdom</u> will be assured to him after he recognizes that it is <u>heaven</u> that <u>rules</u>."

Daniel 4:27 WHAT is Daniel's advice to Nebuchadnezzar? "Break away now from your <u>sins</u> by doing <u>righteousness</u>. Show <u>mercy</u> to the <u>poor</u>."

(100) ELICIT DISCUSSION: Does this sound like good news or bad news for King Nebuchadnezzar?

It's good news because he will not lose his kingdom forever. It will be given back to him when he recognizes God's sovereignty.

---

84   WEEK FOUR

Daniel 4:25 Until WHEN? WHAT is King Nebuchadnezzar to recognize?

"That the ___**Most**___ ___**High**___ is ___**ruler**___ over the realm of ___**mankind**___ and ___**bestows**___ it on whomever He ___**wishes**___."

Daniel 4:26 WHY is the stump with the roots of the tree left?

To show Nebuchadnezzar that his ___**kingdom**___ will be assured to him after he recognizes that it is ___**heaven**___ ___ that ___**rules**___.

Daniel 4:27 WHAT is Daniel's advice to Nebuchadnezzar?

"Break away now from your ___**sins**___ by doing ___**righteousness**___ Show ___**mercy**___ to the ___**poor**___."

Does this sound like good news or bad news for King Nebuchadnezzar? ___ Good ___ Bad

(100) Wow! Can you believe this dream? God starts off showing Nebuchadnezzar how awesome his kingdom is. The tree is strong and fruitful. Then God shows him that he will be driven from mankind until he recognizes that there is a Most High, the Ruler of mankind, who bestows power on whomever He wishes.

Daniel gives the king great advice: "Break away from your sins and do righteousness." God is giving the king a chance to change his ways and his heart and to recognize that God is the Giver of his kingdom. All that he has is from the Most High. There is a Ruler over all, and it's not King Nebuchadnezzar. It's El Elyon—God Most High!

Cut and print! Now use all the words from each of the blanks on pages 82-84 and circle them in the word search on the next page. If a word is used more than once, you only need to circle it one time.

101

A Vision of a Strong Tree 85

```
N D k S H R M A J E S T Y N
E E u q u O P P D S M R E S
V M B x W L S P O E i V N S
i R D U P E T A M H E i A E
R A N i C S L L N S Z N S
D L i k W H q E i W i S T H U
Y A k P E O A E i W P M i O
k i N G D O M D O N T E G U E
B E A S T S M T N H G R H O E
R P M G R A S S E E C D E T H
S D O i R E P x i A Z Y R H G
H V C R B O N C T V R Z A i G
A R T A O V R U L E R T A i
E q E R i S T R O N G J H R
```

Way to go! We are so proud of you! Will Nebuchadnezzar change? Will he break away from his sins? You'll find out. Don't forget to practice your memory verse.

Guided Instruction

101 Find the words underlined on pages 82-84 in the Word Search on page 85 and circle them.

Practice saying your memory verse three times with a friend.

Guided Instruction

Day
Four

King Nebuchadnezzar is still proud. He does not believe he has to change. Do you believe you don't have to change?

Ask God to give you a special message from His Word today.

102 Turn to page 85 and read "Scene Four: Babylon the Great."

Review key words on page 74.

God (Most High, King of heaven) (draw a purple triangle and color it yellow)

Daniel (Belteshazzar) (color it blue)

Dream (vision) (draw a blue cloud around it)

Nebuchadnezzar (color it orange)

Kingdom (draw a purple crown and color it blue)

Sin (iniquities) (color it brown)

Where (double-underline words that denote place in green)

When (draw a green clock over words that denote time)

103 Turn to page 150 and read Daniel 4:28-33 aloud using your Observation Worksheet visual aid as students follow along and call out each key word. Then mark them together as we noted on page 37.

DAY FOUR

(page 85)

102 ### SCENE FOUR: BABYLON THE GREAT

You did a wonderful job helping Miss Anna out yesterday. Today we have a very cool assignment for you. You get to help Mr. Jackson, the makeup artist, get Nebuchadnezzar transformed for a very unbelievable scene. But before you head to the makeup room, turn to page 150.

---

86   WEEK FOUR

Read Daniel 4:28-33 and mark the key words listed on page 74 in these verses or use your key-word bookmark.

Don't forget to mark your pronouns! And mark anything that tells you WHERE by double-underlining the WHERE in green. Mark anything that tells you WHEN by drawing a green clock 🕐 or green circle like this: ◯.

Now that ~~your~~ ~~scripts~~ are marked, ask the 5 W's and an H.

---

prolonging of your prosperity.'   (page 150)

103 28 "All this happened to Nebuchadnezzar the king.

29 " Twelve months later he was walking on the roof of the royal palace of Babylon.

30 "The king reflected and said, 'Is this not Babylon the great, which I myself have built as a royal residence by the might of my power and for the glory of my majesty?'

31 "While the word was in the king's mouth, a voice came from heaven, saying, 'King Nebuchadnezzar, to you it is declared: sovereignty has been removed from you,

32 and you will be driven away from mankind, and your dwell-

Observation Worksheets   151

ing place will be with the beasts of the field. You will be given grass to eat like cattle, and seven periods of time will pass over you until you recognize that the Most High is ruler over the realm of mankind and bestows it on whomever He wishes.'

33 "Immediately the word concerning Nebuchadnezzar was fulfilled; and he was driven away from mankind and began eating grass like cattle, and his body was drenched with the dew of heaven until his hair had grown like eagles' feathers and his nails like birds' claws.

(page 86)

...ck or green circle like this.

Now that your scripts are marked, ask the 5 W's and an H. After that you can show WHAT happens to King Nebuchadnezzar by drawing the storyboards for these two scenes.

Daniel 4:29-30 WHAT was King Nebuchadnezzar saying as he walked around the roof of his palace?

"Is this not ___Babylon___ the great, which I myself have ___built___ as a royal ___residence___ by the might of my ___power___ and for the ___glory___ of my ___majesty___?"

Take a look at Miss Anna's production notes in the box to see why King Nebuchadnezzar was so proud of his city and palace.

(104)

PRODUCTION MANAGER'S NOTES

Babylon the Great

Did you know that Babylon covered 20 square miles? It had two gigantic walls to protect it. The inner wall was so wide that two chariots could fit side by side. Babylon could be entered through eight different gates. The most famous gate was the northern Ishtar Gate, which was decorated with dragons and bulls in enameled bricks. And the road to this gate had high walls that were decorated with lions. Inside this gate was the main palace that Nebuchadnezzar built.

The city of Babylon was famous for its hanging gardens that

A Vision of a Strong Tree   87

*Nebuchadnezzar built for one of his queens who was home-sick for her country. These hanging gardens are one of the seven wonders of the world. Nebuchadnezzar was the greatest king of the neo-Babylonian period and the last great ruler of Babylon.**

WHOM is Nebuchadnezzar praising for all he has? Circle one:

   a. God   (b.) Himself

Daniel 4:31 WHAT does the voice from heaven say?

"___Sovereignty___ has been ___removed___ from you."

Guided Instruction

Read the selected verses to answer the questions.

Daniel 4:29-30 WHAT was King Nebuchadnezzar saying as he walked around the roof of his palace? "Is this not <u>Babylon</u> the great, which I myself have <u>built</u> as a royal <u>residence</u> by the might of my <u>power</u> and for the <u>glory</u> of my <u>majesty</u>?"

(104) Read the "Production Manager's Notes" about Babylon.

WHOM is Nebuchadnezzar praising for all he has? (b.) Himself

Daniel 4:31 WHAT does the voice from heaven say? "<u>Sovereignty</u> has been <u>removed</u> from you."

Guided Instruction

105 Draw a sketch from Daniel 4:28-32 for the storyboard scene in the box on page 87.

Daniel 4:33 WHAT happened? <u>King Nebuchadnezzar was driven from mankind. The Word concerning him was fulfilled</u>.

106 Draw a sketch from Daniel 4:33 for the storyboard scene in the box on page 88.

Practice saying your memory verse three times with a friend.

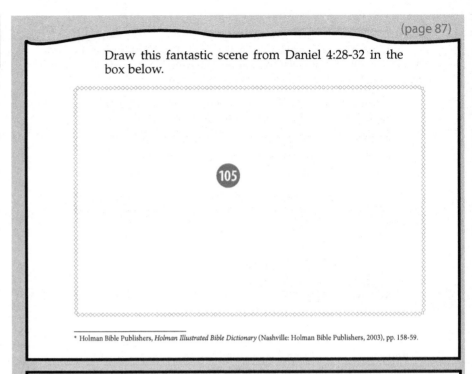

(page 87)

Draw this fantastic scene from Daniel 4:28-32 in the box below.

105

* Holman Bible Publishers, *Holman Illustrated Bible Dictionary* (Nashville: Holman Bible Publishers, 2003), pp. 158-59.

88   WEEK FOUR

Daniel 4:33 WHAT happened? Did Nebuchadnezzar's dream come true? Was he driven from mankind? Did he lose his reason and his kingdom for seven periods of time?

<u>King Nebuchadnezzar was driven from mankind.</u> <u>The Word concerning him was fulfilled.</u>

Draw this very unusual and amazing scene of Daniel 4:33 in the box below.

106

(page 88)

Wow! Can you believe it? God gave Nebuchadnezzar 12 months from the time Daniel interpreted his dream to turn from his sins. What a patient God! But WHAT does Nebuchadnezzar do? Instead of recognizing WHO God is, he shows his pride in all his accomplishments, his kingdom, and his power.

Nebuchadnezzar had built an awesome kingdom of beautiful hanging gardens, gigantic walls decorated with lions, and

---

A Vision of a Strong Tree   89

gates decorated with dragons and bulls. Twelve months later we see Nebuchadnezzar walking around on the roof of the palace and bragging about what an awesome palace and kingdom he has built.

But God showed him WHO the King really is. Immediately Nebuchadnezzar was driven from mankind, eating grass like the cattle. WHAT will happen next? Will King Nebuchadnezzar be driven from mankind for the rest of his life, eating grass like the cattle, having hair like eagles' feathers, and sporting nails like birds' claws? You'll find out. Don't forget to practice your memory verse!

Guided Instruction

Guided Instruction

God is patient but King Nebuchadnezzar was proud and did not turn from his sins.

Ask God to show you His will for your life. Ask Him to give you understanding as you study His Word.

107 Turn to page 89 and read "Scene Five: A Humbled King."

Review key words on page 74.

God (Most High, King of heaven) (draw a purple triangle and color it yellow)

Daniel (Belteshazzar) (color it blue)

Dream (vision) (draw a blue cloud around it)

Nebuchadnezzar (color it orange)

Kingdom (draw a purple crown and color it blue)

Sin (iniquities) (color it brown)

Where (double-underline words that denote place in green)

When (draw a green clock over words that denote time)

108 Turn to page 151 and read Daniel 4:34-37 aloud using your Observation Worksheet visual aid as students follow along and call out each key word. Then mark them together as we noted on page 37.

(page 89)

107

SCENE FIVE: A HUMBLED KING

"Thanks, Aunt Sherry, for letting us help Mr. Jackson transform King Nebuchadnezzar into a beast with hair like eagles' feathers and nails like birds' claws," Molly said as Aunt Sherry walked up.

Max joined in. "That was the coolest. It is so amazing how makeup can transform a man into a beast. We are having a great time."

"Well, I'm proud of you for all your hard work marking scripts, running lines, and especially for studying God's Word. Are you ready to find out what happens to King Nebuchadnezzar?"

"We sure are!" Max and Molly laughed as they spoke at the same time.

---

90   WEEK FOUR

"Great! I'll pray and then we'll pull out our scripts."

Turn to page 151. Read Daniel 4:34-37 and mark your key words listed on page 74 in these verses or use your key-word bookmark.

Don't forget to mark your pronouns! And mark anything that tells you WHEN by drawing a green clock 🕐 or green circle like this: ◯ .

---

nails like birds' claws.

108 34 "But at the end of that period, I, Nebuchadnezzar, raised my eyes toward heaven and my reason returned to me, and I blessed the Most High and praised and honored Him who lives forever;
For His dominion is an everlasting dominion,
And His kingdom endures from generation to generation.
35 "All the inhabitants of the earth are accounted as nothing,
But He does according to His will in the host of heaven
And among the inhabitants of earth;
And no one can ward off His hand
Or say to Him, 'What have You done?'

(page 151)

Or say to Him, 'What have You done?'

36 "At that time my reason returned to me. And my majesty and splendor were restored to me for the glory of my kingdom, and my counselors and my nobles began seeking me out; so I was reestablished in my sovereignty, and surpassing greatness was added to me.

37 "Now I, Nebuchadnezzar, praise, exalt and honor the King of heaven, for all His works are true and His ways just, and He is able to humble those who walk in pride."

(page 90)

Daniel 4:34 WHEN did Nebuchadnezzar have his reason return to him?

At the end of that period, when he blessed the Most High and praised and honored Him

Daniel 4:36 WHAT did God restore to Nebuchad-nezzar?

His reason, His majesty and splendor were restored to him. His sovereignty was reestablished.

Daniel 4:37 WHY did God cause Nebuchadnezzar to lose his reason and his kingdom? WHAT is God able to do?

He lost his reason because he believed he built his kingdom by himself. God humbles those who walk in pride.

Draw this scene from Daniel 4:34-37 in the box below.

Guided Instruction

Read the selected verses to answer the questions.

Daniel 4:34 WHEN did Nebuchadnezzar have his reason return to him? At the end of that period, when he blessed the Most High and praised and honored Him

Daniel 4:36 WHAT did God restore to Nebuchadnezzar? His reason, His majesty and splendor were restored to him. His sovereignty was reestablished.

Daniel 4:37 WHY did God cause Nebuchadnezzar to lose his reason and his kingdom? WHAT is God able to do? He lost his reason because he believed he built his kingdom by himself. God humbles those who walk in pride.

109 Draw a sketch from Daniel 4:34-37 for the storyboard scene in the box on page 90.

Guided Instruction

List things you learned about God in Daniel 4:32-37 on page 91.

What I Learned About God

Daniel 4:32 God is the Most High. He is ruler over the realm of mankind and bestows it on whomever He wishes. He is Sovereign.

Daniel 4:34 He lives forever. His dominion is an everlasting dominion. His kingdom endures from generation to generation.

Daniel 4:35 He does according to His will in the host of heaven and among the inhabitants on the earth.

Daniel 4:37 He is the King of heaven. All His works are true and His ways are just. He is able to humble those who walk in pride.

 Draw a picture in the box on page 91 that shows everything that God is over.

A Vision of a Strong Tree   91

Make a list of the things you learned about God in Daniel 4:32-37.

> **What I Learned About God**
>
> **Daniel 4:32** God is the Most High. He is ruler over the realm of mankind and bestows it on whomever He wishes. He is Sovereign.
>
> **Daniel 4:34** He lives forever. His dominion is an everlasting dominion. His kingdom endures from generation to generation.
>
> **Daniel 4:35** He does according to His will in the host of heaven and among the inhabitants on the earth.
>
> **Daniel 4:37** He is the King of heaven. All His works are true and His ways are just. He is able to humble those who walk in pride.

WHAT an *awesome* God! Look at verse 35 and see all that God is over. He is over the host of heaven and all the inhabitants of the earth. Draw a picture in the box below to show everything that God is over.

Amazing! God is over *everything!* Nebuchadnezzar was driven from mankind for seven periods of time until he raised his eyes to heaven to recognize, bless, and praise God Most High!

Nebuchadnezzar was humbled. He finally got it. Nebuchadnezzar finally saw who God is: not just another god, not just Daniel's God, but El Elyon, God Most High and Ruler over everything. And God restored to him the glory of his kingdom.

God is the only One to be worshiped and praised. In Isaiah 42:8, God says He will not give His glory to another. God created us. He gives us our gifts and abilities. We are not to brag about the things we do. We are to give God the honor and glory.

HOW about you? Do you honor and praise God—or yourself? Do you brag about your sports ability, about how smart and talented you are, or about your looks? Write out the gifts that God has given you and tell how you handle those gifts. Also tell if there is anything you need to change.

_____

_____

_____

_____

Remember: God humbles those who walk in pride. Don't be like Nebuchadnezzar. Praise God for all that He has given you! Every good and perfect gift comes from God (James 1:17).

Awesome work! Don't forget to say your memory verse out loud to a grown-up, and ask that person if he or she sees any pride in you. If the grown-up says yes, go to God and ask Him to help you be humble like Daniel.

Guided Instruction

111 ELICIT DISCUSSION about gifts God has given each one.

112 Write about these gifts and about what you need to change.

If you are a classroom teacher you may want to give your students a quiz on their memory verse. There is also a quiz on Week Four on page 156 to check memory and understanding.

Play the *Drawing Game* on page 162 to review all the kids have learned.

Guided Instruction

WEEK 5

DAY ONE

You read about Nebuchadnezzar, the arrogant king who finally turned to God after He dealt hard with him. Since then, he has died.

And now a wicked king is on the stage. How will God deal with him?

Ask God to keep you humble and lead you to a clear understanding of His Word.

113 Turn to page 93 and read "Daniel 5" and "A Change of King."

5

HANDWRITING ON THE WALL

113

DANIEL 5

What an amazing week as we filmed a very arrogant and proud king driven from mankind, eating grass like the cattle, with hair like eagles' feathers and nails like birds' claws. Mr. Jackson did an awesome job as he made up King Nebuchadnezzar. Were you surprised to see this mighty king finally humble himself before God Most High? Have you humbled yourself and thanked God for all the gifts He has given you? Way to go! We are so proud of you! What will happen in our new episode this week? Let's head back to the set to find out.

DAY ONE

A CHANGE OF KING

"Come on in," Miss Lenyer called out to Max and Molly. "Did Sherry tell you about the awesome scene we will be filming today?"

"No," replied Max. "We have to mark our scripts to find out."

Miss Lenyer laughed at Max's answer. "All right, you and

93

94   WEEK FIVE

Molly better get started. You don't want to miss this incredible scene."

Let's ask God for His help. Then we need to turn to page 152. Read Daniel 5:1-6 and mark the key words listed below on your Observation Worksheets. Add any new key words to your key-word bookmark.

Key Words for Daniel 5

God (Most High God, Lord) (draw a purple triangle and color it yellow)

Belshazzar (color it pink)

vessels (color it yellow)

Daniel (color it blue)

kingdom (draw a purple crown and color it blue)

Don't forget to mark your pronouns! And mark anything that tells you WHERE by double-underlining the WHERE in green. Mark anything that tells you WHEN by drawing a green clock or green circle like this: ◯.

Now that ~~~~~~~~ are marked, let's film our next scene.

---

152   *Observation Worksheets*

Chapter 5

1 Belshazzar the king held a great feast for a thousand of his nobles, and he was drinking wine in the presence of the thousand.

2 When Belshazzar tasted the wine, he gave orders to bring the gold and silver vessels which Nebuchadnezzar his father had taken out of the temple which was in Jerusalem, so that the king and his nobles, his wives and his concubines might drink from them.

3 Then they brought the gold vessels that had been taken out of the temple, the house of God which was in Jerusalem; and the king and his nobles, his wives and his concubines drank from them.

4 They drank the wine and praised the gods of gold and silver, of bronze, iron, wood and stone.

5 Sudd~~~~~~~~~~~ of a man's h~~~~~~~~~~~~ began

Guided Instruction

114 Turn to page 152 and copy key word markings above the chapter heading. Then copy the markings to your bookmark.

God (Most High God, Lord) (draw a purple triangle and color it yellow)

Belshazzar (color it pink)

vessels (color it yellow)

Daniel (color it blue)

Kingdom (draw a purple crown and color it blue)

Where (double-underline words that denote place in green)

When (draw a green clock over words that denote time)

115 Read Daniel 5:1-6 aloud using your Observation Worksheet visual aid as students follow along and call out each key word. Then mark them together as we noted on page 37.

Guided Instruction

Read the selected verses to answer the questions.

Daniel 5:1 WHO is the king? WHAT's the king's name? Belshazzar

116 Read the "Production Manager's Notes" on page 95 about King Belshazzar.

(page 152)

5 Suddenly the fingers of a man's hand emerged and began writing opposite the lampstand on the plaster of the wall of the king's palace, and the king saw the back of the hand that did the writing.

6 Then the king's face grew pale and his thoughts alarmed him, and his hip joints went slack and his knees began knocking together.

(page 94)

Now that your scripts are marked, let's film our next scene.

Daniel 5:1 WHO is the king? WHAT's the king's name?

Belshazzar

We have a new king of Babylon. King Nebuchadnezzar died in 562 BC. It is now 539 BC, and Daniel is around 80 years old. Take a look at Miss Anna's background information on this new king, Belshazzar.

Handwriting on the Wall   95

116

PRODUCTION MANAGER'S NOTES

BELSHAZZAR

Did you know that the mention of this king, Belshazzar, used to make some people think that the Bible was not true because they could not find a king of Babylon listed in history named Belshazzar?

Historical accounts listed Nabondius as the last king of Babylon, but the Bible listed a king named Belshazzar. Guess what happened? In the nineteenth century there was an archaeological dig that proved that God's Word was right. There were inscriptions that showed there was a king of Babylon named Belshazzar.

So WHO is Belshazzar? Belshazzar was the son of Nabondius, who became king of Babylon in 556 BC. Because Nabondius was more interested in historical research than in ruling Babylon, he appointed his son Belshazzar as his co-regent. That means they shared being king of Babylon.

(page 95)

In Daniel 5 you will see Nebuchadnezzar referred to as Belshazzar's father. Most scholars believe this is because it was proper (court etiquette) to call Belshazzar the son of King Nebuchadnezzar, even though he was not Belshazzar's father. Belshazzar was a legal heir of King Nebuchadnezzar and is regarded as "the son." Also, in ancient Oriental languages the word FATHER was used to refer to any male ancestor. Remember, Belshazzar's father is Nabondius, his co-regent.*

---
* John Phillips and Jerry Vines, *Exploring the Book of Daniel* (Neptune, NJ: Loizeaux Brothers, 1990), pp. 79, app. 16.

96   WEEK FIVE

Now that we know something about our new king, help Mr. Andy get the props in place so we can start filming our new episode.

Daniel 5:1 WHAT is happening? WHAT is King Belshazzar holding?

A g r e a t f e a s t

Daniel 5:2-3 WHAT does Belshazzar order to be brought to the feast for the king, his nobles, his wives, and his concubines to drink from?

Gold and silver vessels

WHERE were these vessels from?

The Temple in Jerusalem

Daniel 5:4 WHAT did they do as they drank from these holy vessels of God?

They praised gods of gold, silver, bronze, iron, wood, and stone.

Now think about this for a minute. These vessels are the ones that King Nebuchadnezzar brought out of God's temple when he captured Jerusalem. These vessels belonged to the Most High God and were used for temple worship, and here these people are partying, praising the false gods of gold, silver, bronze, iron, wood, and stone.

HOW do you think God feels about His vessels being used to praise another god?

_____

_____

Guided Instruction

Daniel 5:1 WHAT is happening? WHAT is King Belshazzar holding? A g r e a t f e a s t

Daniel 5:2-3 WHAT does Belshazzar order to be brought to the feast for the king, his nobles, his wives, and his concubines to drink from? Gold and silver vessels

WHERE were these vessels from? The Temple in Jerusalem

Daniel 5:4 WHAT did they do as they drank from these holy vessels of God? They praised gods of gold, silver, bronze, iron, wood, and stone.

Guided Instruction

Daniel 5:5 WHAT happened? <u>The fingers of a man's hand began writing a message on the wall.</u>

117 Draw a picture of this event in the box on page 97.

Daniel 5:6 HOW did the king react? <u>He grew pale; thoughts alarmed him; his hip joints went slack and his knees began knocking together.</u>

Handwriting on the Wall   97

Daniel 5:5 WHAT happened?
The fingers of a man's hand began writing a message on the wall.

Draw a picture of this shocking event in the box below.

117

Daniel 5:6 HOW did the king react?
He grew pale; thoughts alarmed him; his hip joints went slack and his knees began knocking together.

Wow! Does this scene give you a clue to how God felt about the king using His holy vessels to praise false gods? Tomorrow we will find out how treating God's vessels as holy applies to you.

Now discover your memory verse for this week by looking at the handwriting on the wall that Miss Lenyer helped Max and Molly create using the inverse alphabet code on the next page.

To decode this message, find the letter of the alphabet that represents the letter written

WEEK FIVE

98

in the message. The first letter in our message on the wall is the letter *Y*. Look at the inverse alphabet code under the letter *Y* and write the letter that *Y* is representing, which is the letter *B*, on the line under the message on the wall. Do the same thing for each letter until you have uncovered God's message, your memory verse for this week. Then find the reference by reading Daniel 5.

Inverse Alphabet Code

A B C D E F G H I J K L M N O P Q R S T U V W X Y Z
| | | | | | | | | | | | | | | | | | | | | | | | | |
Z Y X W V U T S R Q P O N M L K J I H G F E D C B A

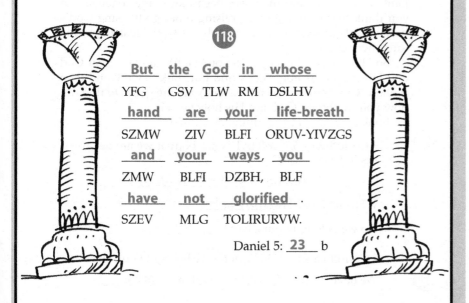

118

But	the	God	in	whose
YFG	GSV	TLW	RM	DSLHV

hand	are	your	life-breath
SZMW	ZIV	BLFI	ORUV-YIVZGS

and	your	ways,	you
ZMW	BLFI	DZBH,	BLF

have	not	glorified
SZEV	MLG	TOLIRURVW.

Daniel 5: __23__ b

Way to go! Now practice this verse three times today!

Guided Instruction

118 Decode the Memory Verse on page 98. Then copy the verse to an index card.

"But the God in whose life-breath and your ways, you have not glorified."

Daniel 5:23b

Practice saying the memory verse three times, three times each day.

Guided Instruction

God does not smile on insults to His holy vessels. Do you think King Belshazzar will get away with this?

Ask God to remind you to glorify Him in all you do. Ask Him to lead as you study His Word.

119 Turn to page 99 and read "God's Holy Vessels."

120 Read the selected verses in 1 Corinthians to answer the questions.

1 Corinthians 6:19 WHAT is our body if we are believers in Jesus Christ? A temple of the Holy Spirit

WHO is in us? The Holy Spirit

Do we belong to ourselves? No.

1 Corinthians 6:20 WHY don't we belong to ourselves? We have been bought with a price.

121 ELICIT DISCUSSION about what this means.

Handwriting on the Wall   99

119

GOD'S HOLY VESSELS

Yesterday was a little scary as we watched King Belshazzar throw a huge party and use God's holy vessels to praise false gods of gold, silver, bronze, iron, wood, and stone.

HOW did God react? A hand appeared and began writing on the wall of the king's palace. Look at King Belshazzar's reaction: His face grew pale, his thoughts alarmed him, his hip joints went slack, and his knees began knocking together. Do you think that drinking and praising other gods using God's holy vessels is treating God as holy, as God Most High, the Ruler over everything?

So HOW does this apply to you? HOW can you treat God and His vessels as holy? Let's find out. Talk to God, and then pull out your script, your Bible. Today we are going to find out how you can honor God and His holy vessels.

Look up and read 1 Corinthians 6:19-20.

120   1 Corinthians 6:19 WHAT is our body if we are believers in Jesus Christ?

_____**A temple of the Holy Spirit**_____

WHO is in us? **The Holy Spirit**

Do we belong to ourselves? ____**No.**____

1 Corinthians 6:20 WHY don't we belong to ourselves?

121   We have been ___**bought**___ with a ___**price**___.

Do you know what that price is? It's Jesus' death on a cross to save us from our sins. Once we accept Jesus Christ as our

Savior, we no longer belong to ourselves. Our bodies are a temple of God, a holy vessel for Him to use.

(122)   Have you accepted Jesus Christ as your Savior? If you haven't invited Jesus into your life and you want to, the first thing you need to do is believe that Jesus is our Savior, that He is God's Son. He is God, and He lived a perfect life without sin and died on a cross to pay for our sins. Then He was buried, and God raised Him from the dead.

You also have to know that you are a sinner and be willing to confess those sins to God and turn away from them. You have to be willing to turn your entire life over to God and to follow Jesus.

You can pray a prayer like this:

> *Thank You, God, for loving me and sending Your Son, Jesus Christ, to die for my sins. I am sorry for the things I have done wrong. I am repenting, changing my mind about my sins. Sin is wrong. I don't want to do things my way anymore. I want to receive Jesus Christ as my Savior, and now I turn my entire life over to You. Amen.*

If you prayed this prayer, you are a part of God's family! You are God's child, and Jesus and the Holy Spirit will come to live in you (John 14:23). You are a temple of the Holy Spirit. You belong to God!

Now look back at 1 Corinthians 6:20. WHAT are we to do?

_____**Glorify**_____ God in your _____**body**_____.

To glorify God is to honor and praise Him. Think about it. You are a holy vessel of God. HOW do you live? Do you praise God with your life, or

Guided Instruction

(122) Read the text on page 100 and see if there are children who want to pray the prayer.

1 Corinthians 6:20 WHAT are we to do?
Glorify God in your body.

Guided Instruction

123 Read over the questions for self-examination with the children. After reading each question, give students time to write responses on pages 101 and 102.

Thank God for the privilege to know Him by studying His Word.

---

102   WEEK FIVE

Tell how you use your feet:

_____

123 "HOW do I dress my body?" If you are a girl, do you dress in short skirts and shirts that show too much? If you are a guy, do you wear shirts that say inappropriate things and jeans that barely stay on?

Does how you dress show other people that you belong to Jesus?

_____

Name one way you can keep God's temple (your body) holy:

_____

Way to go! We are so proud of you.

WHAT will happen when we head back to the set tomorrow? Will there be anyone who can tell King Belshazzar what this hand has written on the wall? We'll find out. Don't forget to practice your memory verse!

(page 102)

DAY THREE

(124)

CALL IN THE WISE MEN

Hey, it's great to have you back on the set! You did a fantastic job yesterday as you learned how to keep God's holy vessel, your body, holy. Today you need to help Mr. Jackson get Belshazzar ready as we film his next scene. Remember what he looked like as we left him in Daniel 5:6? Apply Belshazzar's makeup.

Then turn to page 152. Read Daniel 5:7-12 and mark the key words on page 94 listed in these verses or use your key-word bookmark. Don't forget to mark your pronouns!

Ready on the set! Let's film our next scene.

(page 153)

together.

(125) 7 The king called aloud to bring in the conjurers, the Chaldeans and the diviners. The king spoke and said to the wise men of Babylon, "Any man who can read this inscription and explain its interpretation to me shall be clothed with purple and have

Observation Worksheets 153

a necklace of gold around his neck, and have authority as third ruler in the kingdom."

8 Then all the king's wise men came in, but they could not read the inscription or make known its interpretation to the king.

9 Then King Belshazzar was greatly alarmed, his face grew even paler, and his nobles were perplexed.

10 The queen entered the banquet hall because of the words of the king and his nobles; the queen spoke and said, "O king, live forever! Do not let your thoughts alarm you or your face be pale.

11 "There is a man in your kingdom in whom is a spirit of the holy gods; and in the days of your father, illumination, insight and wisdom like the wisdom of the gods were found in him. And King Nebuchadnezzar, your father, your father the king, appointed him chief of the magicians, conjurers, Chaldeans and diviners.

12 "This was because an extraordinary spirit, knowledge and insight, interpretation of dreams, explanation of enigmas and solving of difficult problems were found in this Daniel, whom the king named Belteshazzar. Let Daniel now be summoned and he will declare the interpretation."

13 Th... ...spoke

Guided Instruction

DAY THREE

Ask God to help you understand what He wants you to do. He is with you in this study.

(124) Turn to page 102 and read "Call in the Wise Men."

Review key words on page 94.

God (Most High God, Lord) (draw a purple triangle and color it yellow)

Belshazzar (color it pink)

vessels (color it yellow)

Daniel (color it blue)

Kingdom (draw a purple crown and color it blue)

Where (double-underline words that denote place in green)

When (draw a green clock over words that denote time)

(125) Turn to page 152 and read Daniel 5:7-12 aloud using your Observation Worksheet visual aid as students follow along and call out each key word. Then mark them together as we noted on page 37.

Guided Instruction

Read the selected verses to answer the questions.

Daniel 5:7 WHOM did the king call for?
Conjurers, Chaldeans, and diviners

WHAT did the king offer the one who could interpret the inscription? "He shall be clothed with purple and have a necklace of gold...and have authority as third ruler."

Daniel 5:8 Could the king's wise men interpret the inscription? No.

Daniel 5:9 HOW did this affect King Belshazzar? He was greatly alarmed; his face grew paler.

HOW did his nobles react? They were perplexed.

Daniel 5:10 WHO enters the banquet hall? The queen

Daniel 5:10-12 WHOM did the queen tell Belshazzar to summon? Daniel

---

Handwriting on the Wall   103

Daniel 5:7 WHOM did the king call for?
Conjurers, Chaldeans, and diviners

WHAT did the king offer the one who could interpret this inscription?

"He shall be clothed with ___purple___ and have a ___necklace___ of ___gold___ ... and have authority as ___third ruler___."

Why third ruler? Remember, there are already two rulers: King Belshazzar and his father, King Nabondius.

Daniel 5:8 Could the king's wise men interpret the inscription?

No.

Daniel 5:9 HOW did this affect King Belshazzar?
He was greatly alarmed; his face grew paler.

(We need more makeup, Mr. Jackson!)

HOW did his nobles react?
They were perplexed.

Daniel 5:10 WHO enters the banquet hall?
The queen

Daniel 5:10-12 WHOM did the queen tell Belshazzar to summon?
Daniel

WHAT do we learn about Daniel in verses 11-12? Make a list in the box on the next page.

WEEK FIVE

What I Learned About Daniel

Daniel 5:11 The Chaldeans believe he has "the spirit of the holy gods." Appointed chief of the magicians, conjurers, Chaldeans, and diviners.

They believe he has illumination, insight, and wisdom like "the wisdom of the gods."

Daniel 5:12 He has extraordinary spirit, knowledge, and insight.

He can interpret dreams.

He can explain enigmas.

He can solve difficult problems.

Named Belteshazzar by King Nebuchadnezzar

Amazing! Will Daniel interpret the handwriting on the wall? Hang in there! You'll find out. Don't forget to practice your memory verse.

Guided Instruction

126 List what you learn about Daniel in verses 11-12 in the box on page 104.

What I learned about Daniel

Daniel 5:11 The Chaldeans believe he has "the spirit of the holy gods." Appointed chief of the magicians, conjurers, Chaldeans, and diviners.

They believe he has illumination, insight, and wisdom like "the wisdom of the gods."

Daniel 5:12 He has extraordinary spirit, knowledge, and insight.

He can interpret dreams.

He can explain enigmas.

He can solve difficult problems.

Named Belteshazzar by King Nebuchadnezzar

Guided Instruction

Day Four

Turn to page 104 and read "Send for Daniel."

Ask God to impress upon you Daniel's character, integrity, and life. Ask Him to glorify Himself through you.

Review key words on page 94.

God (Most High God, Lord) (draw a purple triangle and color it yellow)

Belshazzar (color it pink)

vessels (color it yellow)

Daniel (color it blue)

Kingdom (draw a purple crown and color it blue)

Where (double-underline words that denote place in green)

When (draw a green clock over words that denote time)

127 Turn to page 153 and read Daniel 5:13-23 aloud using your Observation Worksheet visual aid as students follow along and call out each key word. Then mark them together as we noted on page 37.

(page 104)

DAY FOUR

SEND FOR DANIEL

"That was so cool watching the scene where Miss Lenyer made the hand write on the wall," Molly told Max as they headed to the makeup room to tell Mr. Jackson that Aunt Sherry was ready for Daniel.

"It sure was. Hey, Mr. Jackson," Max called out, "Aunt Sherry is ready for Daniel on the set."

"He's ready to go. How does he look?"

"Wow!" Molly exclaimed. "I can't believe it. He really looks 80 years old."

Mr. Jackson smiled. "It's the magic of Hollywood. We can make you look beautiful, old, or transform you into a monster."

Max and Molly laughed at Mr. Jackson's theatrics. "We'll go tell Aunt Sherry that Daniel is on his way."

All right! Quiet on the set everyone. Let's pray so we can

Handwriting on the Wall   105

find out what happens when Daniel comes in to see King Belshazzar. WHAT will Daniel say to this king?

Turn to page 153. Read Daniel 5:13-23 and mark the key words listed on page 94 in these verses or use your key-word bookmark.

Don't forget to mark your pronouns! And mark anything that tells you WHERE by double-underlining the WHERE in green. Mark anything that tells you WHEN by drawing a green clock or green circle like this: ◯.

---

he will declare the interpretation.

(page 153)

127 13 Then Daniel was brought in before the king. The king spoke and said to Daniel, "Are you that Daniel who is one of the exiles from Judah, whom my father the king brought from Judah?

14 "Now I have heard about you that a spirit of the gods is in you, and that illumination, insight and extraordinary wisdom have been found in you.

15 "Just now the wise men and the conjurers were brought in before me that they might read this inscription and make its

(page 154)

interpretation known to me, but they could not declare the interpretation of the message.

16 "But I personally have heard about you, that you are able to give interpretations and solve difficult problems. Now if you are able to read the inscription and make its interpretation known to me, you will be clothed with purple and wear a necklace of gold around your neck, and you will have authority as the third ruler in the kingdom."

17 Then Daniel answered and said before the king, " Keep your gifts for yourself or give your rewards to someone else; however, I will read the inscription to the king and make the interpretation known to him.

18 "O king, the Most High God granted sovereignty, grandeur, glory and majesty to Nebuchadnezzar your father.

19 "Because of the grandeur which He bestowed on him, all the peoples, nations and men of every language feared and trembled before him; whomever he wished he killed and whomever he wished he spared alive; and whomever he wished he elevated and whomever he wished he humbled.

20 "But when his heart was lifted up and his spirit became so proud that he behaved arrogantly, he was deposed from his royal throne and his glory was taken away from him.

21 "He was also driven away from mankind, and his heart was made like that of beasts, and his dwelling place was with the wild donkeys. He was given grass to eat like cattle, and his body was drenched with the dew of heaven until he recognized that

(page 155)

the Most High God is ruler over the realm of mankind and that He sets over it whomever He wishes.

22 "Yet you, his son, Belshazzar, have not humbled your heart, even though you knew all this,

23 but you have exalted yourself against the Lord of heaven; and they have brought the vessels of His house before you, and you and your nobles, your wives and your concubines have been drinking wine from them; and you have praised the gods of silver and gold, of bronze, iron, wood and stone, which do not see, hear or understand. But the God in whose hand are your life-breath and your ways, you have not glorified.

24 "Then the hand was sent from Him and this inscription was

Guided Instruction

Guided Instruction

Read the selected verses to answer the questions.

Daniel 5:13 WHAT does Belshazzar ask Daniel? Are you that Daniel that my father brought from Judah?

Daniel 5:14-16 List some of the things Belshazzar says about Daniel.

The spirit of the gods is in you.

You have illumination, insight, and wisdom.

Daniel 5:17 WHAT will the king give Daniel if he interprets the message? Purple (royal) clothing; a necklace of gold; authority as the third ruler of the kingdom.

Daniel 5:17 HOW does Daniel respond to the king's offer? Keep your gifts; I will interpret the message.

Daniel 5:18-21 WHAT does Daniel remind Belshazzar about? His father lost his kingdom because of pride and arrogance.

Daniel 5:22 WHAT does Daniel tell Belshazzar? You knew all this but did not humble your heart.

Daniel 5:23 WHAT did Belshazzar do wrong? He exalted himself before God. He drank from vessels of the house of God.

In WHOSE hand is Belshazzar's life-breath? God's

WHOM did he not glorify with his ways? God

(page 105)

Daniel 5:13 WHAT does Belshazzar ask Daniel?

Are you that Daniel that my father brought from Judah?

Daniel 5:14-16 List some of the things Belshazzar says about Daniel.

The spirit of the gods is in you.

You have illumination, insight, and wisdom.

Daniel 5:16 WHAT will the king give Daniel if he interprets the message?

Purple (royal) clothing; a necklace of gold; authority as the third ruler of the kingdom.

Daniel 5:17 HOW does Daniel respond to the king's offer?

Keep your gifts; I will interpret the message.

Isn't that awesome? Daniel will tell him the truth, but not for his own personal benefit, not to increase his wealth or to advance himself. Daniel is still a man of faith, wisdom, and integrity.

---

106   **WEEK FIVE**

Daniel 5:18-21 WHAT does Daniel remind Belshazzar about?

His father lost his kingdom because of pride and arrogance.

Daniel 5:22 WHAT does Daniel tell Belshazzar?

You knew all this but did not humble your heart.

Daniel 5:23 WHAT did Belshazzar do wrong?

He exalted himself before God. He drank from vessels of the house of God.

In WHOSE hand is Belshazzar's life-breath? God's

WHOM did he not glorify with his ways? God

(page 106)

128 Wow! Just look at what Daniel says to King Belshazzar. Daniel reminds Belshazzar about what happened when King Nebuchadnezzar became proud. He tells him, "You knew all this, and you still did not humble your heart. You didn't learn from King Nebuchadnezzar's mistakes. You put yourself above God. You drank out of God's vessels and praised other gods. You did not glorify God, even though He holds your breath, your very life in His hands."

Now ask yourself, "Do I honor God with the way I live? Do I realize that every breath I take is in His hands, that my life is a gift from God?"

Name one way you can honor and bless God:

129 _____

How would you like to be given this message? It doesn't sound like the message from the handwriting on the wall is going to be good news, does it? WHAT will God reveal to this king? We'll find out tomorrow.

Guided Instruction

128 ELICIT DISCUSSION about ways students can honor and bless God.

129 Have students write individual responses on page 106.

Guided Instruction

DAY FIVE

Ask God to keep you from being proud and arrogant. Read God's Word with a heart for Him.

130 Turn to page 107 and read "Mene, Mene, Tekel, Upharsin."

Review key words on page 94.

God (Most High God, Lord) (draw a purple triangle and color it yellow)

Belshazzar (color it pink)

vessels (color it yellow)

Daniel (color it blue)

Kingdom (draw a purple crown and color it blue)

Where (double-underline words that denote place in green)

When (draw a green clock over words that denote time)

131 Turn to page 155 and read Daniel 5:24-31 aloud using your Observation Worksheet visual aid as students follow along and call out each key word. Then mark them together as we noted on page 37.

Handwriting on the Wall   107

DAY FIVE

130

MENE, MENE, TEKEL, UPHARSIN

Are you ready to film our last scene this week? WHAT will the handwriting on the wall reveal to this arrogant king? Let's find out. Don't forget to talk to God.

Turn to page 155. Read Daniel 5:24-31 and mark the key words listed on page 94 in these verses or use your key-word bookmark.

Don't forget to mark your pronouns! And mark anything that tells you WHEN by drawing a green clock 🕐 or green circle like this: ◯ .

(page 155)

131 ...e breath and your ways, you have not glorified.

24 "Then the hand was sent from Him and this inscription was written out.

25 "Now this is the inscription that was written out: 'MENĒ, MENĒ, TEKĒL, UPHARSIN.'

26 "This is the interpretation of the message: 'MENĒ'—God has numbered your kingdom and put an end to it.

27 "'TEKĒL'—you have been weighed on the scales and found deficient.

28 "'PERĒS'—your kingdom has been divided and given over to the Medes and Persians."

29 Then Belshazzar gave orders, and they clothed Daniel with purple and put a necklace of gold around his neck, and issued a proclamation concerning him that he now had authority as the third ruler in the kingdom.

30 That same night Belshazzar the Chaldean king was slain.

(page 156)

31 So Darius the Mede received the kingdom at about the age of sixty-two.

(page 107)

Daniel 5:24 WHO sent the hand that wrote the inscription?

God

Daniel 5:25-28 WHAT three things did the inscription tell Belshazzar?

1) "___**God**___ has __**numbered**__ your __**kingdom**__ and put an ___**end**___ to it."

---

108   WEEK FIVE

2) "You have been ___**weighed**___ on the **scale** and found ___**deficient**___."

3) "Your ___**kingdom**___ has been ___**divided**___ and given over to the ___**Medes**___ and __**Persians**__."

Whoa! How would you like to get a message like this? God is very, very upset with King Belshazzar. God tells Belshazzar his kingdom is over. He has been found deficient. Belshazzar's kingdom will be divided and given to the Medes and the Persians. Remember Nebuchadnezzar's dream about the statue? Do you remember how God told him he was the head of gold but another kingdom, an inferior kingdom, would take over? Does it sound like that is about to happen?

Daniel 5:29 WHAT happened to Daniel?

He was clothed in purple, given a necklace of gold, and given the authority of "third ruler."

Daniel 5:30 WHAT happened to Belshazzar? WHEN did it happen?

That same night, he was slain.

Daniel 5:31 WHO receives the kingdom?

Darius the Mede

Guided Instruction

Read the selected verses to answer the questions.

Daniel 5:24 WHO sent the hand that wrote the inscription? God

Daniel 5:25-28 WHAT three things did the inscription tell Belshazzar? "God has numbered your kingdom and put an end to it."

"You have been weighed on the scale and found deficient."

"Your kingdom has been divided and given over to the Medes and Persians."

Daniel 5:29 WHAT happened to Daniel? He was clothed in purple, given a necklace of gold, and given the authority of "third ruler."

Daniel 5:30 WHAT happened to Belshazzar? WHEN did it happen? That same night, he was slain.

Daniel 5:31 WHO receives the kingdom? Darius the Mede

Guided Instruction

ELICIT DISCUSSION: **Is Nebuchadnezzar's dream about the statue coming true?** <u>Yes</u>.

Daniel 5:28 WHOM does it say Belshazzar's kingdom is given over to?" <u>Medes and Persians</u>

Turn back to page 49 and write **"<u>Kingdom of the Medes and Persians</u>"** beside the silver breast and arms of the statue.

WHAT does chapter 5 show us about King Belshazzar?

c. He was arrogant.

d. He didn't know or honor God.

e. He mocked God.

f. He was proud.

g. He placed himself above God by praising other gods with God's holy vessels.

Ask yourself, "Am I more like Belshazzar or Daniel?" Write your response on the line on page 109.

Do you live to please God?

Handwriting on the Wall   109

132 Is Nebuchadnezzar's dream about the statue coming true?

Yes.

Look at Daniel 5:28. WHOM does it say Belshazzar's kingdom is given over to?

Medes and Persians

God has just shown you the next kingdom on the statue! Why don't you turn back to your picture of the statue on page 49 and in the space next to the silver breast and arms write the name of the next kingdom: Kingdom of Medes and Persians. Isn't that exciting!

Now WHAT does chapter 5 show us about King Belshazzar? Circle all of the descriptions below that you think apply to him.

a. He was humble.   b. He was a great king.

c. He was arrogant.   d. He didn't know or honor God.

e. He mocked God.   f. He was proud.

g. He placed himself above God by praising other gods with God's holy vessels.

Belshazzar did not learn from King Nebuchadnezzar's mistakes. He thought he was invincible, that nothing could touch him because he was ruling such an awesome kingdom. But Belshazzar found out there is a God who holds man's breath in His hand, and He alone is to be praised.

134 Ask yourself, "Am I more like Belshazzar or Daniel?"

"Do I think I can do whatever I want to? Or do I live to please God?" Write out what you do, and give an

110   WEEK FIVE

(135) example of how you are living to have your way or how you're living to please God:

_____

_____

_____

_____

_____

_____

    All right! As you leave the set this week, don't forget to say your memory verse to a grown-up. Ask God to show you when you are walking in pride, and to help you glorify Him in all your ways!

Guided Instruction

(135) Do you live to please God? On page 110 write out how you are living to please God.

What a blessing! You have enjoyed the privilege of studying about God.

If you are a classroom teacher you may want to give your students a quiz on their memory verse. There is also a quiz on Week Five on page 157 to check memory and understanding.

Now, play a game so the kids can review all they have learned.

Guided Instruction

WEEK 6

DAY ONE

Daniel ran into a lot of personal enemies. King Darius's commissioners were jealous of Daniel and meant to do him harm. Who do you think came to his rescue?

Ask God to keep you in His care and help you trust Him more. He will be with you during this study. Let your heart be filled with this realization.

136 Turn to page 111 and read "Daniel 6" and "Cast Change."

6

CAST INTO THE LIONS' DEN

136

DANIEL 6

Wow! What did you think about King Belshazzar and that scary handwriting on the wall with its message of doom for this king? Would you ever dishonor God the way he did? Remember, we are God's holy vessels. Our lives are to praise Him!

Are you ready to find out what happens to Daniel next? Let's head back to the set and find out what happens with the new king.

DAY ONE

CAST CHANGE

"Okay! Places, everybody. Is Darius ready for our next scene?" Aunt Sherry called out. "Good. Bring him out. Okay, Mr. Grayson, we'll start with Camera Two. We're ready to roll. Quiet on the set! Let's pray. Stand by…action!"

Turn to page 156, to our opening scene. Read Daniel 6:1-5 and mark the key words listed on the next page in your Observation Worksheets. Add any new key words to your key-word bookmark.

111

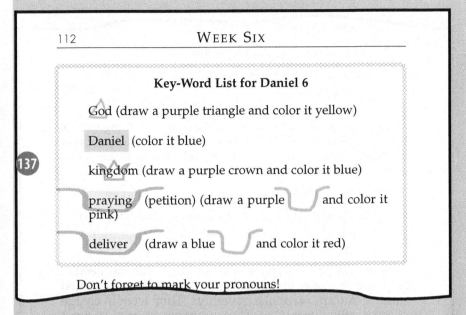

112   WEEK SIX

Key-Word List for Daniel 6

God (draw a purple triangle and color it yellow)

Daniel (color it blue)

kingdom (draw a purple crown and color it blue)

praying (petition) (draw a purple ⌣ and color it pink)

deliver (draw a blue ⌣ and color it red)

Don't forget to mark your pronouns!

Chapter 6   (page 156)

1 It seemed good to Darius to appoint 120 satraps over the kingdom, that they would be in charge of the whole kingdom,

2 and over them three commissioners (of whom Daniel was one), that these satraps might be accountable to them, and that the king might not suffer loss.

3 Then this Daniel began distinguishing himself among the commissioners and satraps because he possessed an extraordinary spirit, and the king planned to appoint him over the entire kingdom.

4 Then the commissioners and satraps began trying to find a ground of accusation against Daniel in regard to government affairs; but they could find no ground of accusation or evidence of corruption, inasmuch as he was faithful, and no negligence or corruption was to be found in him.

5 Then these men said, "We will not find any ground of accusation against this Daniel unless we find it against him with regard to the law of his God."

6 Then these commissioners and satraps came by agreement to the king and spoke to him as follows: "King Darius, live forever!

7 "All the commissioners of the kingdom, the prefects and the

---

Guided Instruction

137 Turn to page 156 and copy the key word markings above the chapter heading as well as on your bookmark.

God (draw a purple triangle and color it yellow)

Daniel (color it blue)

Kingdom (draw a purple crown and color it blue)

Praying (petition) (draw a purple bowl and color it pink)

Deliver (draw a blue bowl and color it red)

Where (double-underline every word that denotes place in green)

When (draw a blue clock over every word that denotes time)

138 Read Daniel 6:1-5 aloud using your Observation Worksheet visual aid as students follow along and call out each key word. Then mark them together as we noted on page 37.

Guided Instruction

Read the selected verses to answer the questions.

Daniel 6:1-2 WHO is the king? Darius the Mede

Daniel 6:2 HOW does Darius set up the kingdom? He appoints 120 satraps over the kingdom and he puts three commissioners over these satraps.

WHO is one of the three commissioners? Daniel

Daniel 6:3 HOW well did Daniel do his job? He distinguished himself.

WHAT did the king plan to appoint Daniel over? The entire kingdom

Daniel 6:4 WHAT did these other commissioners and satraps do? They tried to find something against Daniel.

(page 112)

Don't forget to mark your pronouns!

Now WHO is in our opening scene?

Daniel 6:1-2 WHO is the king?
Darius the Mede

Remember, we saw Darius take over the kingdom of Babylon in Daniel 5:30-31. The head of gold has fallen, and now the Medes and Persians (the breast and arms of silver) are in control of Babylon.

Daniel 6:2 HOW does Darius set up the kingdom?

He appoints __120__ __satraps__ over the kingdom and he puts t_h_r_e_e c_o_m_m_i_s_s_i_o_n_e_r_s over these satraps.

King Darius' kingdom was so large that he needed help to watch over his people and wealth. So he appointed satraps. Satraps were like governors. They were in charge of areas called provinces. The satraps reported to commissioners. Commissioners were like vice presidents. They made sure the satraps did their jobs, and they managed large areas, probably made up of many provinces. The

---

Cast into the Lions' Den   113

king would be like a president…except he wasn't elected! He was sovereign and could do anything he wanted to.

WHO is one of the three commissioners?
Daniel

Remember, Daniel is over 80 years old.

Daniel 6:3 HOW well did Daniel do his job?
He distinguished himself.

WHAT did the king plan to appoint Daniel over?
The entire kingdom

Amazing! Daniel does such an awesome job that the king is going to set him over the entire kingdom. Let's find out how the other commissioners and satraps feel about that.

Daniel 6:4 WHAT did these other commissioners and satraps do?
They tried to find something against Daniel.

Have you ever been jealous of any of your friends when something good happened to them? (Circle one) Yes   No
HOW did you behave? Were you happy? Did you tell them how great they did? Or did you put them down or talk about them behind their backs? Did you wish it were you?

(page 113)

them behind their backs? Did you wish it were you?

Write out what you did:

_____

139

Daniel 6:4-5 Did these commissioners and satraps find anything wrong to accuse Daniel of?

No. _____

Why don't you make a list of the things you learned about Daniel in verses 3-5 in the box on the next page?

---

114   WEEK SIX

What I Learned About Daniel

Daniel 6:3 He distinguished himself among the commissioners and satraps.

140 He possessed an extraordinary spirit.

Daniel 6:4 No grounds for accusations

No evidence of corruption

Faithful

141 Wow! Just look at Daniel! He is 80 years old, and he hasn't changed. After some people become great, they become proud. But not Daniel. These commissioners and satraps can't find anything to accuse Daniel of. First, we see there is no corruption. That means there is no bad or wicked behavior in Daniel. Remember what we learned about Daniel's character in Week One on page 32. Daniel has integrity. He is honest, trustworthy, and sincere. He does the right thing, even when no one is looking.

Now take a moment and ask yourself, "Is there anything in my life that I have done where someone could say something bad about me? Can they accuse me of telling a lie, of cheating on a test, or of stealing something?" If there is anything someone could accuse you of, write out what they could say about you.

What did you say or do?

_____

Now ask God to forgive you. Way to go!

Look at what else the commissioners and satraps say about Daniel. He is faithful. There is no negligence in him. "No negligence" means Daniel did what was required of him. He was very careful in his job. He gave it his very best!

HOW do you do your work? Your work would include chores your parents give you like cleaning the kitchen, cleaning your room, and putting away your clothes and things. It would also include your work at school.

Guided Instruction

139 ELICIT DISCUSSION:

Have you ever been jealous of any of your friends?

HOW did you behave? Write out your response.

Daniel 6:4 Did these commissioners and satraps find anything wrong to accuse Daniel of? <u>No.</u>

140 LIST things you learned about Daniel in verses 3-5 in the box on page 114.

What I Learned About Daniel

Daniel 6:3 <u>He distinguished himself among the commissioners and satraps.</u>

<u>He possessed an extraordinary spirit.</u>

Daniel 6:4 <u>No grounds for accusations</u>

<u>No evidence of corruption</u>

<u>Faithful</u>

141 Read the rest of the text on pages 114-115. ELICIT DISCUSSION and give students time to respond independently.

Guided Instruction

Write out HOW you do your work. Do you do what you are asked to do? Are you careful? Do you give it your very best? Or are you sloppy and do just enough to get by? Write out WHAT you do:

_____

_____

HOW do your actions show your character? For example, you might write, "I show I try my best when I study for a test and hand in my homework."

_____

_____

_____

All right! You have done a fantastic job! Tomorrow we will find out what these commissioners and satraps do, since they can't find anything to accuse Daniel of. But before you leave the set, you need to uncover this week's memory verse.

Take a look at the awesome lions' den scene on the next page. Unscramble the words underneath the blanks in this scene to complete your verse and find out what King Darius has to say about the God of Daniel. Then look at Daniel 6 to find the reference.

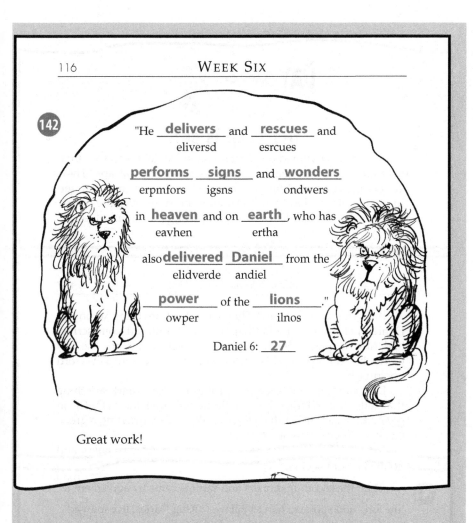

116   WEEK SIX

"He __delivers__ and __rescues__ and
　　　eliversd　　　esrcues

__performs__　__signs__　and __wonders__
erpmfors　　igsns　　　　ondwers

in __heaven__ and on __earth__, who has
　　eavhen　　　　　ertha

also __delivered__　__Daniel__ from the
　　elidverde　　andiel

__power__　of the　__lions__."
owper　　　　　　ilnos

Daniel 6: __27__

Great work!

Guided Instruction

142 Turn to page 116 and unscramble the words to find the memory verse.

"He **delivers** and **rescues** and

performs **signs** and **wonders**

in **heaven** and on **earth**, who has

also **delivered** **Daniel** from the

power of the **lions**." Daniel 6:**27**

Copy the Memory Verse to an index card and practice saying it three times, three times daily.

Guided Instruction

Ask God to lead you as you study His Word. He has a special message for you today.

143 Turn to page 116 and read "The Trap is Set!"

Review key words on page 112.

God (Most High God, Lord) (draw a purple triangle and color it yellow)

Belshazzar (color it pink)

vessels (color it yellow)

Daniel (color it blue)

Kingdom (draw a purple crown and color it blue)

Where (double-underline words that denote place in green)

When (draw a green clock over words that denote time)

144 Turn to page 156 and read Daniel 6:6-10 aloud using your Observation Worksheet visual aid as students follow along and call out each key word. Then mark them together as we noted on page 37.

DAY TWO

(page 116)

THE TRAP IS SET!

143 Yesterday we filmed our first scene in Daniel 6 and saw that there are some very jealous commissioners and satraps. They are looking for something to accuse Daniel of so they can get rid of him. They don't want Daniel to be ruler over the entire kingdom. They want the power and prestige for themselves.

Cast into the Lions' Den   117

But what can they do? They can't find anything wrong in Daniel. Let's find out what happens next. Pull out your scripts and turn to page 156. Read Daniel 6:6-10 and mark the key words listed on page 112 in these verses or use your key-word bookmark.

Don't forget to mark your pronouns! And mark anything that tells you WHERE by double-underlining the WHERE in green. Mark anything that tells you WHEN by drawing a green clock 🕐 or green circle like this: ○ .

~~to the law of his God."~~

(page 156)

144 6 Then these commissioners and satraps came by agreement to the king and spoke to him as follows: "King Darius, live forever!

7 "All the commissioners of the kingdom, the prefects and the satraps, the high officials and the governors have consulted together that the king should establish a statute and enforce an

(page 157)

injunction that anyone who makes a petition to any god or man besides you, O king, for thirty days, shall be cast into the lions' den.

8 "Now, O king, establish the injunction and sign the document so that it may not be changed, according to the law of the Medes and Persians, which may not be revoked."

9 Therefore King Darius signed the document, that is, the injunction.

10 Now when Daniel knew that the document was signed, he entered his house (now in his roof chamber he had windows open toward Jerusalem); and he continued kneeling on his knees three times a day, praying and giving thanks before his God, as he had been doing previously.

11 Then these by agreement and found Daniel

Now roll those cameras. What are our commissio— satraps up to?

Daniel 6:6-7 WHAT plot do these commissioners and satraps come up with? WHAT statute and injunction (law) do they propose to the king?

"Anyone who makes a **petition** to any **god** or **man** besides **you**, O king, for **thirty** days, shall be **cast** into the **lions' den**."

Daniel 6:8 WHAT do we find out happens to this document if it is signed?

It becomes law and cannot be revoked according to the law of the Medes and Persians.

Did you know that a decree written into law by the Medes and Persians could not be changed? Why do you think this document would please King Darius? Could it be because these commissioners and satraps appeal to the king's pride? Look at how they start out in verse 6 with some praise: "King Darius, live forever!" Then there is the clincher: "If you make this statute, no one can ask anything

118   WEEK SIX

of any other man or god but you for 30 days." Look at how they went straight for the king's ego: "You will be the one everyone will come to."

Daniel 6:9 Does Darius sign this document?
Yes.

The trap has been set. WHAT will Daniel do?

Daniel 6:10 WHAT does Daniel do once he knows this document is signed?
He kneels down and prays to God three times a day.

Daniel knows that this document means that if he prays, he

Guided Instruction

Read the selected verses to answer the questions.

Daniel 6:6-7 WHAT plot do these commissioners and satraps come up with? WHAT statute and injunction (law) do they propose to the king?
"Anyone who makes a petition to any god or man beside you, O king, for thirty days, shall be cast into the lions' den."

Daniel 6:8 WHAT do we find out happens to this document if it is signed? It becomes law and cannot be revoked according to the law of the Medes and Persians.

Daniel 6:9 Does Darius sign this document? Yes.

Daniel 6:10 WHAT does Daniel do once he knows this document is signed? He kneels down and prays to God three times a day.

Guided Instruction

WHAT did Daniel do? He continued underline{praying} on his knees.

HOW many times a day? Three

Does he hide in his room? Let's see, it says, "His w i n d o w s were open."

Did he whine or complain, "Why is this happening to me?" WHAT does it say in verse 10? He gave t h a n k s before God.

145 ELICIT DISCUSSION:

WHO is in control? God

Do you pray every day? Do you thank God even when bad things happen?

146 Give students time to reflect and respond on page 119.

Practice saying the Memory Verse with a friend.

(page 118)

Daniel knows that this document means that if he prays, he will end up in the lions' den. Is he afraid? Does he say, "I won't pray. After all, it's only for 30 days. God will understand. He won't want me to be thrown in the lions' den"? No. Daniel does what?

He continued __praying__ on his knees. HOW many times a day? Three

Does he hide in his room? Let's see, it says, "His w i n d o w s were open," which means he could probably be seen and heard outside.

Did he whine or complain, "Why is this happening to me"? WHAT does it say in verse 10? He gave t h a n k s before God.

145 Wow! Daniel is brave. He does not fear man. Daniel is faithful to God. He knows WHO is in control of his circumstances! Even though something bad has happened, Daniel continues to pray just like he has always done each and every day. HOW did Daniel pray? Daniel thanks God.

Cast into the Lions' Den   119

146 HOW about you? Do you pray every day, or do you let other things get in the way?

_____

Do you thank God even when bad things happen to you?

_____

WHAT will happen to Daniel? Darius has signed a document that cannot be changed. Will Daniel be thrown into the lions' den for praying? Don't forget to say your memory verse today!

(page 119)

DAY THREE

(147)

A DISTRESSED KING

"Okay—places, everyone," Aunt Sherry called out. "Are our commissioners and satraps ready? Good. Olivia, check the king's costume. All right. Now we're ready. Quiet on the set. Stand by. Roll Camera Two, Mr. Grayson. And action."

Don't forget to pray. Then turn to page 157. Read Daniel 6:11-18 and mark the key words listed on page 112 in these verses or use your key-word bookmark.

Don't forget to mark your pronouns! And mark anything that tells you WHERE by double-underlining the WHERE in green. Mark anything that tells you WHEN by drawing a green clock

(page 157)

...he had been doing previously.

(148)

11 Then these men came by agreement and found Daniel making petition and supplication before his God.

12 Then they approached and spoke before the king about the king's injunction, "Did you not sign an injunction that any man who makes a petition to any god or man besides you, O king, for thirty days, is to be cast into the lions' den?" The king replied, "The statement is true, according to the law of the Medes and Persians, which may not be revoked."

13 Then they answered and spoke before the king, "Daniel, who is one of the exiles from Judah, pays no attention to you, O king, or to the injunction which you signed, but keeps making his petition three times a day."

14 Then, as soon as the king heard this statement, he was deeply

---

158 *Observation Worksheets*

distressed and set his mind on delivering Daniel; and even until sunset he kept exerting himself to rescue him.

15 Then these men came by agreement to the king and said to the king, "Recognize, O king, that it is a law of the Medes and Persians that no injunction or statute which the king establishes may be changed."

16 Then the king gave orders, and Daniel was brought in and cast into the lions' den. The king spoke and said to Daniel, "Your God whom you constantly serve will Himself deliver you."

17 A stone was brought and laid over the mouth of the den; and

---

Guided Instruction

DAY THREE

Ask God to show you how to respond when someone is trying to accuse you of something.

147 Turn to page 119 and read "A Distressed King."

Review key words on page 112.

God (Most High God, Lord) (draw a purple triangle and color it yellow)

Daniel (color it blue)

Kingdom (draw a purple crown and color it blue)

Praying (petition) (draw a purple bowl and color it pink)

Deliver (draw a blue bowl and color it red)

Where (double-underline words that denote place in green)

When (draw a green clock over words that denote time)

148 Turn to page 157 and read Daniel 6:11-18 aloud using your Observation Worksheet visual aid as students follow along and call out each key word. Then mark them together as we noted on page 37.

Guided Instruction

Read the selected verses to answer the questions.

Daniel 6:11 WHAT do the men find Daniel doing? Making petition and supplication before his God

Daniel 6:12 WHAT did they remind the king about? His signed injunction

Daniel 6:13 WHAT did they tell the king about Daniel? "Daniel, who is one of the exiles from Judah, pays no attention to you, or to the injunction which you signed, but keeps making his petition three times a day."

Daniel 6:14 HOW does the king react to hearing this about Daniel? He's distressed and wants to rescue Daniel.

Daniel 6:15 Could the king deliver Daniel? WHAT do we see about the law of the Medes and the Persians? He could not deliver Daniel; the law of the Medes and Persians cannot be changed.

Daniel 6:16 WHAT happens to Daniel? He's cast into the lions' den.

WHO does the king say will deliver Daniel? "Your God will deliver you."

(page 158)

God whom you constantly serve will Himself deliver you."

17 A stone was brought and laid over the mouth of the den; and the king sealed it with his own signet ring and with the signet rings of his nobles, so that nothing would be changed in regard to Daniel.

18 Then the king went off to his palace and spent the night fasting, and no entertainment was brought before him; and his sleep fled from him.

19 Then the king arose at dawn, at the break of day, and went in

(page 119)

mark anything with a clock ⏰ or green circle like this: ◯.

Now come in close. Let's find out what happens to Daniel.

Daniel 6:11 WHAT do the men find Daniel doing? Making petition and supplication before his God

Daniel 6:12 WHAT did they remind the king about? His signed injunction

Daniel 6:13 WHAT did they tell the king about Daniel?

" Daniel , who is one of the exiles from Judah, pays no attention to you, or to the injunction which you signed, but keeps making his petition three times a day."

Daniel 6:14 HOW does the king react to hearing this about Daniel? He's distressed and wants to rescue Daniel.

Daniel 6:15 Could the king deliver Daniel? WHAT do we see about the law of the Medes and the Persians? He could not deliver Daniel; the law of the Medes and Persians cannot be changed.

Daniel 6:16 WHAT happens to Daniel? He's cast into the lions' den.

WHO does the king say will deliver Daniel? "Your God will deliver you."

(page 120)

Daniel 6:17 WHAT was laid over the den, and HOW was it sealed?

<u>A stone was laid over the den, and the den was sealed with the king's signet ring.</u>

Daniel 6:18 HOW did the king spend his night?

<u>Fasting, no entertainment</u>
<u>and sleep</u>

Cast into the Lions' Den   121

149   Just look at how the king desperately tries to find a way to save Daniel, but because of his pride in signing a document that can't be changed, there is nothing he can do. He tells Daniel, "The God you constantly serve will deliver you." Then he goes off and spends the night fasting for Daniel.

Pretty amazing that a pagan king would care about what happens to one of his captives enough to go without sleep, food, or entertainment. This shows us once again how awesome Daniel is.

WHAT will the king find in the morning? Hang in there. We'll find out tomorrow! Don't forget to practice your memory verse!

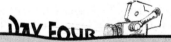

DAY FOUR

Guided Instruction

Daniel 6:17 WHAT was laid over the den, and HOW was it sealed? <u>A stone was laid over the den, and the den was sealed with the king's signet ring.</u>

Daniel 6:18 HOW did the king spend his night? <u>Fasting, no entertainment and sleep</u>

149 ELICIT DISCUSSION: WHAT will the king find in the morning?

Guided Instruction

DAY FOUR

150 Turn to page 121 and read "Sleeping With The Lions."

Ask God to help you understand how Daniel could be in such trouble and still not be afraid.

Review key words on page 112.

God (Most High God, Lord) (draw a purple triangle and color it yellow)

Daniel (color it blue)

Kingdom (draw a purple crown and color it blue)

Praying (petition) (draw a purple bowl and color it pink)

Deliver (draw a blue bowl and color it red)

Where (double-underline words that denote place in green)

When (draw a green clock over words that denote time)

151 Turn to page 158 and read Daniel 6:19-23 aloud using your Observation Worksheet visual aid as students follow along and call out each key word. Then mark them together as we noted on page 37.

(page 121)

DAY FOUR

150 **SLEEPING WITH THE LIONS**

"Wow!" Max exclaimed as he and Molly walked onto the set and saw Mr. Leon, the animal trainer, working with the lions.

"Come on over," Mr. Leon called out, "and meet the lions.

122   WEEK SIX

We're about ready to shoot their big scene. When we're finished, I'll let you give them their treat."

Molly smiled. "They look pretty hungry to me. What if they think we're their treat?" Mr. Leon laughed. "Don't worry. I'll be right there with you."

Aunt Sherry walked up. "Everything looks good to go, Mr. Leon. I'm going to open with Camera Three on the lions, so get them ready to growl and pace around Daniel. Then we'll go to Camera Two where the camera will open wide and pan around Daniel."

"Got it," Mr. Leon answered as he snapped his whip. "Come on, fellows. We're ready for action."

Wow! Are you amazed at how huge these hungry lions are? WHAT did King Darius find the next morning after Daniel spent the night with these ferocious beasts? Let's find out.

Turn to page 158. Read Daniel 6:19-23 and mark the key words listed on page 112 in these verses or use your key-word bookmark.

Don't forget to mark your pronouns! And mark anything that tells you WHEN by drawing a green clock ⏰ or green circle like this: ◯.

Daniel 6:19 WHEN did the king rise?

(page 158)

151 19 Then the king arose at dawn, at the break of day, and went in haste to the lions' den.

20 When he had come near the den to Daniel, he cried out with a troubled voice. The king spoke and said to Daniel, "Daniel, servant of the living God, has your God, whom you constantly serve, been able to deliver you from the lions?"

21 Then Daniel spoke to the king, "O king, live forever!

22 "My God sent His angel and shut the lions' mouths and they have not harmed me, inasmuch as I was found innocent before Him; and also toward you, O king, I have committed no crime."

23 Then the king was very pleased and gave orders for Daniel

Observation Worksheets   159

to be taken up out of the den. So Daniel was taken up out of the den and no injury whatever was found on him, because he had trusted in his God.

(page 122)

Daniel 6:19 WHEN did the king rise?

At dawn

Did the king take his time checking on Daniel? Give King Darius his directions: Should he walk to the lions' den or run? Circle the correct answer: Walk (Run)

Daniel 6:20 WHAT did Darius's voice sound like?

Troubled

Now give King Darius his lines. WHAT does he say to Daniel?

"Daniel, __**servant**__ of the __**living**__ __**God**__, has your __**God**__, whom you __**constantly**__ __**serve**__, been able to __**deliver**__ you from the __**lion**__?"

Guided Instruction

Read the selected verses to answer the questions.

Daniel 6:19 WHEN did the king rise? <u>At dawn</u>

HOW should the king go to the den? He should <u>run</u>.

Daniel 6:20 WHAT did Darius's voice sound like? <u>Troubled</u>

WHAT does he say to Daniel? "Daniel <u>servant</u> of the <u>living God</u>, has your <u>God</u>, whom you <u>constantly</u> <u>serve</u>, been able to <u>deliver</u> you from the <u>lion</u>?"

Guided Instruction

Daniel 6:21 WHAT does Daniel say? "O king, live forever!"

152 ELICIT DISCUSSION: How would you treat someone who had thrown you into a lions' den? Would you try to get even?

153 Give students time to write responses on page 123.

Daniel 6:22 HOW did Daniel survive this terrible night? WHAT did God do?

154 Draw a picture of the scene in Daniel 6:22 in the box on page 123.

Cast into the Lions' Den   123

Let's put Camera One on the opening to the lions' den. Is there any answer to King Darius's question?

Daniel 6:21 WHAT does Daniel say?
"O king, live forever!"

152 Wow! Are you amazed? Not only is Daniel alive, but listen to his response: "O king, live forever!" In situations like this, a person's true character comes out. Look at the respect Daniel shows the king, who has thrown him into the lions' den. There is no anger, no bitterness, no resentment, just honor and praise.

153 HOW would you treat someone who had just thrown you to the lions? Think about how you would treat one of your friends if he or she hurt your feelings or betrayed you.

Would you still be nice to that person, or would you try to get even?

Daniel 6:22 HOW did Daniel survive this terrible night? WHAT did God do? Draw a picture of this scene that Daniel describes in Daniel 6:22 in the box below.

124   WEEK SIX

HOW was Daniel found before God? (Circle one.)

Guilty    Innocent

Daniel 6:23 HOW did the king react?

He was very ___**pleased**___.

WHY was there no injury found on Daniel?

He had trusted God.

Wow! Can someone say that about you? Can they look at your life and see that you trust God?

_____

Don't forget to practice your memory verse to remind you that God is the One who has the power to deliver and rescue.

Guided Instruction

HOW was Daniel found before God?
<u>Innocent</u>

Daniel 6:23 HOW did the king react?
He was very <u>pleased</u>.

WHY was there no injury found on Daniel? <u>He had trusted God</u>.

155 ELICIT DISCUSSION: Do you trust God? Can anyone look at you and see that you do?

Practice saying the Memory Verse with a friend.

Guided Instruction

DAY FIVE

What do you think should be done to the malicious men who reported Daniel?

Ask God to help you understand the lesson from His Word today.

156 Turn to page 124 and read "The King's New Decree."

Review key words on page 112.

God (Most High God, Lord) (draw a purple triangle and color it yellow)

Daniel (color it blue)

Kingdom (draw a purple crown and color it blue)

Praying (petition) (draw a purple bowl and color it pink)

Deliver (draw a blue bowl and color it red)

Where (double-underline words that denote place in green)

When (draw a green clock over words that denote time)

157 Turn to page 159 and read Daniel 6:24-28 aloud using your Observation Worksheet visual aid as students follow along and call out each key word. Then mark them together as we noted on page 37.

DAY FIVE   (page 124)

156

THE KING'S NEW DECREE

"Hey, Aunt Sherry," Molly said as Sherry walked into the screening room, "we just saw the awesome footage that Mr. Grayson shot of Daniel and the lions. It is so cool! He did a fantastic job with the lions. They were so scary until the angel appeared and Mr. Leon gave them their cue."

Cast into the Lions' Den   125

Aunt Sherry smiled. "That's why we have Mr. Leon. Did you know that in Hollywood they call him the 'animal whisperer,' since he is so good at getting the animals to do what he wants them to do?"

"Hey, Max," Molly grinned and winked at Aunt Sherry, "maybe you should let him work with Sam."

Max petted Sam. "Don't let Molly mess with you. Just look at how good you've been." Everyone cracked up laughing.

"Okay, guys," Aunt Sherry said, "we need to get back to the set. Can you believe that this is the last scene for Season One of our television series? We need to find out what happens to those men who tricked the king into signing that document."

"Oh, man!" Max exclaimed. "That sounds like someone is in trouble to me. I can't believe this is our last day on the set. When will we get to start on Season Two?"

"It won't be long," Aunt Sherry answered. "Just as soon as everyone has a short vacation, we will start filming our next season. It will be incredible! We'll get a glimpse into the future to find out who else has visions and dreams and what they mean."

"All right," Molly said. "I can't wait!"

"Okay, guys, we need to get this season wrapped up. Molly, why don't you pray and then we can get started?"

Are you ready to film our final episode? This is going to be an awesome television series. Let's find out WHAT the king did to those men who maliciously accused Daniel. To be malicious is to want to harm someone out of spite, to have an evil motive.

Turn to page 159. Read Daniel 6:24-28 and mark the key words listed on page 112 in these verses or use your key-word bookmark.

Don't forget to mark your pronouns! And mark anything that tells you WHEN by drawing a green clock or green circle like this: ◯.

157 den and no injury whatever was found on him, because he had trusted in his God. (page 159)

24 The king then gave orders, and they brought those men who had maliciously accused Daniel, and they cast them, their children and their wives into the lions' den; and they had not reached the bottom of the den before the lions overpowered them and crushed all their bones.

25 Then Darius the king wrote to all the peoples, nations and men of every language who were living in all the land: "May your peace abound!

26 " I make a decree that in all the dominion of my kingdom men are to fear and tremble before the God of Daniel;

For He is the living God and enduring forever,

And His kingdom is one which will not be destroyed,

And His dominion will be forever.

27 "He delivers and rescues and performs signs and wonders In heaven and on earth,

Who has also delivered Daniel from the power of the lions."

28 So this Daniel enjoyed success in the reign of Darius and in the reign of Cyrus the Persian.

---

126   WEEK SIX

Look at Daniel 6:24 and draw this scene that shows WHAT the king did to these men who set out to destroy Daniel. Don't forget to also show WHAT happened to their families.

158

Daniel 6:25 WHAT did Darius do next?

Guided Instruction

Read the selected verses to answer the questions.

Daniel 6:24 WHAT did the king do to these men who set out to destroy Daniel? Include WHAT happened to their families. <u>They were all cast into the den and the lions overpowered them and crushed all their bones.</u>

 158 Draw this scene in the box on page 126.

Guided Instruction

Daniel 6:25 WHAT did Darius do next?
Darius the king w r o t e to all the peoples, nations, and men of every language who were living in all the land.

Daniel 6:26 WHAT did he make? A decree

WHAT was this decree? Men are to fear and tremble before the God of Daniel.

Daniel 6:22, 26, 27 WHAT did you learn about God?

What I Learned About God

Daniel 6:22 He sent His angel and shut the lions' mouths.

Daniel 6:26 He is the living God, enduring forever.

His kingdom will not be destroyed.

His dominion will be forever.

Daniel 6:27 He delivers and rescues and performs signs and wonders in heaven and on earth.

He delivered Daniel from the power of the lions.

ELICIT DISCUSSION: Daniel was brave and trusted God.

What will you do when something scary happens to you? Give students time to respond.

Daniel 6:28 WHAT happened to Daniel? He enjoyed success in the reign of Darius the Mede and Cyrus the Persian.

(page 126)

Daniel 6:25 WHAT did Darius do next?

Darius the king w r o t e to all the __peoples__, __nations__, and men of every __language__ who were living in all the land.

Daniel 6:26 WHAT did he make?
A decree

WHAT was this decree?
Men are to fear and tremble before the God of Daniel.

Wow! Look at this awesome decree! Let's make a list in the box on the next page of WHAT you learned about God in Daniel 6:22,26,27.

Cast into the Lions' Den   127

What I Learned About God

Daniel 6:22 He sent His angel and shut the lions' mouths.

Daniel 6:26 He is the living God, enduring forever.

His kingdom will not be destroyed.

His dominion will be forever.

Daniel 6:27 He delivers and rescues and performs signs and wonders in heaven and on earth.

He delivered Daniel from the power of the lions.

WHAT an amazing God! Now that you know that God is the One who has the power to shut the lions' mouths, to deliver and rescue you, should you be afraid when you are in a hard and difficult situation? Will you be brave like Daniel? Will you pray and trust God, even if it means you may end up "thrown into the lions' den"?

Tell what you will do the next time something bad or scary happens to you:

_____

_____

Daniel 6:28 WHAT happened to Daniel?
He enjoyed success in the reign of Darius the Mede and Cyrus the Persian.

(page 127)

Once again we see God's blessing on Daniel's trust and obedience to Him. Think about what Darius said in Daniel 6:20: "your God, whom you constantly serve." WHAT a testimony to be known as someone who constantly serves God. Wow! Daniel never compromises to fit into the world he lives in. Daniel fears

---

128   WEEK SIX

only One, and that One is God. He is a brave man. He is willing to die to love and serve God. What a witness his life has been to these pagan kings.

As you leave the set today, ask yourself, "WHAT kind of witness am I? Do I look and act like everyone else? Or do kids and grown-ups see Jesus in my life when they look at me?"

Write out HOW you are a good witness for Jesus. Do you share Jesus with other kids? Do you turn the other cheek by not getting even if someone is mean to you? Do you help other people? Do you treat others as more important than yourself? Do you stand firm when other people try to sway you?

162   HOW do your actions show Jesus?

_____

_____

All right! Now say your memory verse to a grown-up. WHAT a God! Are you ready to be a Daniel? Cut and print! That was awesome. We are so proud of you!

163   **İT'S A WRAP!**

Way to go! You did it! You have helped film an amazing television series that will show people everywhere just WHO Daniel is and WHAT happens to him. Just look at all you have  learned. You know that God is a sovereign God. His name is El Elyon. He is God Most High. He is in control over all your circumstances! God is in control of EVERYTHING!

You also saw Daniel and his friends get taken into captivity. They lost their homes, their families, their language, and their

---

Guided Instruction

ELICIT A DISCUSSION about the rest of the text.

162 HOW do your actions show Jesus? Respond.

Practice saying your Memory Verse with a friend.

163 Read "It's A Wrap!" on pages 128-129.

What a wonderful study! Thank God for the privilege of being in His Word!

If you are a classroom teacher you may want to give your students a quiz on their memory verse. There is also a quiz on Week Six on page 158 and a final exam on page 159 to check memory and understanding.

Now, grab some props and act out the scenes from Daniel 1-6. Kids love to act out scenes and it reinforces all they have learned.

Guided Instruction

Cast into the Lions' Den   129

---

names. All their hopes and dreams for their lives were changed in a moment.

Yet they never got angry or bitter. They never questioned God. Instead they made up their minds to serve God no matter what the cost. They stood firm when their faith was tested in a fiery furnace and a lions' den. They dared to be different. They were willing to give up their lives to serve the one true God. They were brave men! Are you willing to be brave like Daniel?

You also got to fast-forward into the future as God gave King Nebuchadnezzar a dream of a statue that showed four kingdoms and a stone that crushes those ten toes, the ten kings.

So far you have discovered two of those kingdoms: the kingdom of Babylon and the kingdom of the Medes and Persians. You also saw that the stone represents God's kingdom. God's kingdom will never be destroyed. It crushes all of the kingdoms and endures forever! All right!

WHO are the other two kingdoms on the statue? Just wait. You'll find out, along with some other amazing things that are going to happen in the future. You won't believe it! Wait until you see some of the cool visions and dreams. One is about four ferocious beasts. WHAT does it all mean? Find out when you join us back on the set as we film our second season on the life of Daniel: *Fast-Forward to the Future.*

Don't forget to fill out the card in the back of this book. We have something special that we want to send you for learning to be brave like Daniel. We are so very proud of you! Keep up the good work. See you back on the set to finish our television series on Daniel in God's Word real soon!

Molly, Max, and

(Sam)

D4Y "You're a Brave Man, Daniel" Quizzes

Week 1: Welcome to Babylon...or Modern-Day Iraq

1. Who is king of Babylon at this time?
   a. Nebuchadnezzar
   b. Absalom
   c. David
   d. Solomon

2. Who is king of Judah at this time?
   a. David
   b. Jehoiakim
   c. Solomon
   d. Darius

3. Where does Nebuchadnezzar come to?
   a. Bethel
   b. Damascus
   c. Jerusalem
   d. Susa

4. What did Nebuchadnezzar come to do?
   a. Throw a party
   b. Besiege Jerusalem
   c. Start a business
   d. Collect taxes

5. Who gave King Jehoiakim into King Nebuchadnezzar's hand?
   a. David
   b. Solomon
   c. Darius
   d. God

6. What did King Jehoiakim do?
   a. Evil in the sight of God
   b. Good for the Israelites
   c. Left his palace
   d. Met with Darius

7. What did King Nebuchadnezzar bring to Babylon?
   a. Armies
   b. Articles from the house of the Lord
   c. Food
   d. Weapons

8. Who did King Nebuchadnezzar order to be brought in?
   a. Some of the sons of Israel
   b. His buddies
   c. His armies
   d. His servants

9. What did Daniel make up his mind to do?
   a. Fight for the king
   b. Disobey God
   c. Not eat the king's food
   d. Change his appearance

10. What does God grant Daniel?
    a. A wife
    b. Favor and compassion
    c. Time off for vacation
    d. Time with his friends

Memory Verse

Daniel 1:8

"But Daniel made up his mind that he would not defile himself with the king's choice food or with the wine which he drank; so he sought permission from the commander of the officials that he might not defile himself."

Week 2: The King's Dream

1. What frightened King Nebuchadnezzar?
   a. A war
   b. A dream
   c. King Darius
   d. The sons of Israel

2. What does Nebuchadnezzar want his magicians and sorcerers to do?
   a. Gather the sons of Israel
   b. Throw a party
   c. Interpret his dream
   d. Collect his servants

3. Who do they say are the only ones who can interpret the dream?
   a. Gods who do not dwell with mortal flesh
   b. Gods who dwell with angels
   c. Gods who dwell with men
   d. Angels

4. Who did Daniel say would interpret the dream?
   a. King Darius
   b. A God in heaven who reveals mysteries
   c. Other Israelites
   d. His servants

5. What does God make known to King Nebuchadnezzar?
   a. Who is coming
   b. What is important
   c. What will happen in the future
   d. What Daniel can do

6. What was the dream about?
   a. An army
   b. A cupbearer
   c. A great tree
   d. A great statue

7. What was the head of the statue made of?
   a. Wood
   b. Gold
   c. Silver
   d. Bronze

8. What were the breast and arms made of?
   a. Bronze
   b. Gold
   c. Silver
   d. Iron

9. What were the belly and thighs made of?
   a. Gold
   b. Bronze
   c. Iron
   d. Silver

10. What were the legs made of?
   a. Silver
   b. Bronze
   c. Iron
   d. Gold

Memory Verse

Daniel 2:20-21

"Daniel said, 'Let the name of God be blessed forever and ever, for wisdom and power belong to Him. It is He who changes the times and the epochs. He removes kings and establishes kings; He gives wisdom to wise men and knowledge to men of understanding.'"

Week 3: A Fiery Furnace

1. What did King Nebuchadnezzar make?
   a. An image of gold
   b. Idols of bronze
   c. A feast
   d. Articles for worship

2. What command did the king give to the people?
   a. Come to me
   b. Worship my image
   c. Celebrate with me
   d. Leave the city

3. If they didn't do what he said they would be:
   a. Deported
   b. Rewarded
   c. Cast into a furnace
   d. Sent to war

4. Who did Nebuchadnezzar order to be thrown into the furnace?
   a. Persian kings
   b. All the captives
   c. Shadrach, Meshach, and Abed-nego
   d. Some angels

5. What did they tell the king?
   a. God will deliver us
   b. An army will save us
   c. Daniel will save us
   d. You will lose your kingdom

6. How did the king react to their answer?
   a. Celebrated
   b. Filled with wrath
   c. Dismissed them all
   d. Called for a feast

7. What did Nebuchadnezzar say "the fourth one" in the furnace looked like?
   a. An animal
   b. My servant
   c. A son of the gods
   d. A cupbearer

8. What affect did the fire have on Shadrach, Meshach, and Abed-nego?
   a. They smelled like smoke
   b. Their hair was singed
   c. Their trousers were damaged
   d. No affect on their bodies

9. Why were the boys delivered?
   a. They trusted God
   b. They were brave
   c. They were happy
   d. They were needed

10. What does Nebuchadnezzar say about God?
    a. He is indifferent
    b. No other god is able to deliver this way
    c. He favors boys
    d. He is friendly

Memory Verse

Daniel 3:18

"But even if He does not, let it be known to you, O King, that we are not going to serve your gods or worship the golden image that you have set up."

800 points

1,000 points week 1-3
mem. verses

1. What made Nebuchadnezzar fearful?

Week 4: A Vision of a Strong Tree

   a. Another dream
   b. Daniel
   c. Darius
   d. Meshach

2. Who does Nebuchadnezzar bring into his presence?
   a. Other kings
   b. More Israelites
   c. Wise men
   d. Daniel

3. What is Nebuchadnezzar's second dream about?
   a. An army
   b. A strong tree
   c. Wild animals
   d. His servants

4. What does Daniel see descend from heaven?
   a. An angelic watcher
   b. A choir
   c. Abraham
   d. Joseph

5. What did the one who descended shout out?
   a. Be careful
   b. Watch out
   c. Chop down the tree
   d. Go away

6. What did the tree represent?
   a. Nebuchadnezzar
   b. Darius
   c. David
   d. Solomon

7. Daniel says this tree shows that the king is:
   a. Noble
   b. Great and strong
   c. Arrogant
   d. Immoral

8. What is going to happen to Nebuchadnezzar?
   a. He will prosper
   b. He will get stronger
   c. He will be driven from mankind
   d. He will have another feast

9. What did God do?
   a. Removed King Nebuchadnezzar's sovereignty
   b. Praised the king's strength
   c. Told Daniel to leave the king
   d. Ignored the king's arrogance

10. What does Nebuchadnezzar conclude about God at this time?
   a. He delivers boys from furnaces
   b. He delivered Israel from their captivity
   c. He humbles those who walk in pride
   d. He drives out armies

Memory Verse

Daniel 4:37

"Now, I Nebuchadnezzar, praise, exalt, and honor the king of heaven, for all His works are true and His ways just and He is able to humble those who walk in pride."

Week 5: Handwriting on the Wall

1. Who replaced Nebuchadnezzar?
   a. Belshazzar
   b. Darius
   c. David
   d. Solomon

2. What did this king bring in for his feast?
   a. Food and drinks
   b. Gold and silver vessels
   c. Flowers and palms
   d. Candles and placemats

3. Where were these objects from?
   a. Egypt
   b. The temple in Jerusalem
   c. His palace
   d. The East

4. What happened?
   a. Too many people came
   b. People were rowdy
   c. A human finger wrote a message on a wall
   d. Dancers were late

5. How did the king react?
   a. He was unkind
   b. He was alarmed
   c. He didn't care
   d. He laughed

6. What is our body if we are believers in Jesus Christ?
   a. Well tanned
   b. Healthy and conditioned
   c. A temple of the Holy Spirit
   d. Wonderfully made

7. What did Belshazzar do wrong?
   a. Exalted himself before God
   b. Bowed down to his guests
   c. Ignored the warning
   d. Sent his guests away

8. What did the inscription on the wall tell Belshazzar?
   a. He was a great king
   b. His kingdom is numbered and will end
   c. He will get a medal
   d. He will be honored

9. Who numbered the king's kingdom?
   a. Daniel
   b. Darius
   c. God
   d. Solomon

10. What was the interpretation of the message?
    a. His kingdom will be given to the Medes and the Persians
    b. His kingdom will last forever
    c. There will be a flood
    d. There will be an earthquake

Memory Verse

Daniel 5:23

"But the God in whose hand are your life-breath and your ways you have not glorified."

Week 6: Cast Into the Lions' Den

1. Who appointed Daniel over the entire king-dom?
   a. Darius
   b. Belshazzar
   c. David
   d. Solomon

2. Who became one of the commissioners?
   a. Meshach
   b. Daniel
   c. David
   d. Abed-nego

3. What did the other commissioners do?
   a. Applauded Daniel
   b. Gave Daniel a medal
   c. Tried to accuse Daniel
   d. Ignored Daniel's success

4. If someone prayed to anyone other than the king he would be:
   a. Imprisoned
   b. Cast into the lions' den
   c. Given a robe
   d. Promoted

5. What did Daniel do when he heard about the decree?
   a. Ran away
   b. Hid in the palace
   c. Knelt and prayed to God
   d. Pretended not to know

6. Who was cast into the lions' den?
   a. Daniel
   b. Meshach
   c. Abed-nego
   d. David

7. What did God do?
   a. Killed the king
   b. Shut the lions' mouths
   c. Talked to the king
   d. Ignored Daniel's problem

8. Why was Daniel saved?
   a. He was the favorite.
   b. He was strong.
   c. He trusted God.
   d. He fought the lions.

9. What did King Darius do?
   a. Blessed Daniel
   b. Scoffed at his safety
   c. Decreed that all men tremble at Daniel's God
   d. Left the palace

10. What happened to Daniel?
    a. Enjoyed success
    b. Left the palace
    c. Went back to his family
    d. Was a failure

Memory Verse

Daniel 6:27

"He delivers and rescues and performs signs and wonders in heaven and on earth, who has also delivered Daniel from the power of the lions."

D4Y "You're a Brave Man, Daniel" Final Exam

1. Who is king of Babylon in Daniel I?
   a. Nebuchadnezzar
   b. Absalom
   c. David
   d. Solomon

2. Who is king of Judah in Daniel I?
   a. David
   b. Jehoiakim
   c. Solomon
   d. Darius

3. What did Nebuchadnezzar come to Jerusalem to do?
   a. Throw a party
   b. Start a business
   c. Besiege Jerusalem
   d. Collect taxes

4. What did King Nebuchadnezzar bring to Babylon?
   a. Armies
   b. Articles from the house of the Lord
   c. Food
   d. Weapons

5. Who did King Nebuchadnezzar order to be brought in?
   a. Some of the sons of Israel
   b. His buddies
   c. His armies
   d. His servants

6. What frightened King Nebuchadnezzar?
   a. A war
   b. A dream
   c. King Darius
   d. The sons of Israel

7. Who did Daniel say would interpret the dream?
   a. King Darius
   b. Magicians
   c. A God in heaven who reveals mysteries
   d. His servants

8. What does God make known to King Nebuchadnezzar?
   a. Who is coming
   b. What is important
   c. What will happen in the future
   d. What Daniel can do

9. What was the dream about?
   a. A great statue
   b. An army
   c. A cupbearer
   d. A great tree

10. What was the head of the statue made of?
    a. Wood
    b. Gold
    c. Silver
    d. Bronze

11. What were the breast and arms made of?
    a. Bronze
    b. Gold
    c. Silver
    d. Iron

12. What were the belly and thighs made of?
    a. Gold
    b. Bronze
    c. Silver
    d. Iron

13. What were the legs made of?
    a. Gold
    b. Bronze
    c. Iron
    d. Silver

14. What did King Nebuchadnezzar make?
    a. An image of gold
    b. Idols of bronze
    c. A feast
    d. Articles for worship

15. What command did the king give to the people?
    a. Celebrate with me
    b. Worship my image
    c. Leave the city
    d. Come to me

16. If they didn't do what he said they would be:
    a. Deported
    b. Rewarded
    c. Cast into a furnace
    d. Sent to war

D4Y "You're a Brave Man, Daniel" Final Exam

17. Who was thrown into the furnace?
    a.   Persian kings
    b.   Shadrach, Meshach, and Abed-nego
    c.   All the captives
    d.   Some angels

18. What did they tell the king?
    a.   God will deliver us
    b.   An army will save us
    c.   Daniel will save us
    d.   You will lose your kingdom

19. What did the king say he saw in the furnace with the boys?
    a.   His servant
    b.   A warrior
    c.   Another animal
    d.   One like a son of the gods

20. What is Nebuchadnezzar's second dream about?
    a.   A strong tree
    b.   Wild animals
    c.   An army
    d.   His servants

21. What did the tree represent?
    a.   Darius
    b.   Nebuchadnezzar
    c.   David
    d.   Solomon

22. What did God do?
    a.   Removed King Nebuchadnezzar's sovereignty
    b.   Praised the king's strength
    c.   Told Daniel to leave the king
    d.   Ignored the king's arrogance

23. What did King Belshazzar bring in for his feast?
    a.   Food and drinks
    b.   Gold and silver vessels
    c.   Flowers and palms
    d.   Candles and placemats

24. What happened?
    a.   Too many people came
    b.   People were rowdy
    c.   A human finger wrote a message on a wall
    d.   Dancers were late

25. What did the inscription on the wall tell Belshazzar?
    a.   He was a great king
    b.   He will get a medal
    c.   He will be honored
    d.   His kingdom was numbered and will end

26. If someone prayed to anyone other than the king he would be:
    a.   Imprisoned
    b.   Cast into the lions' den
    c.   Given a robe
    d.   Promoted

27. Who was cast into the lions' den?
    a.   Daniel
    b.   Meshach
    c.   David
    d.   Abed-nego

28. What did God do?
    a.   Killed the king
    b.   Shut the lions' mouths
    c.   Ignored Daniel's problem
    d.   Talked to the king

29. Why was Daniel saved?
    a.   He trusted God
    b.   He was brave
    c.   He was strong
    d.   He was the favorite

30. What did King Darius do?
    a.   Blessed Daniel
    b.   Decreed that all men tremble at Daniel's God
    c.   Left the palace
    d.   Scoffed at Daniel's delivery

Quiz Answer Key

Week 1	Week 2	Week 3	Week 4	Week 5	Week 6
1. a	1. b	1. a	1. a	1. a	1. a.
2. b	2. c	2. b	2. c	2. b	2. b
3. c	3. a	3. c	3. b	3. b	3. c
4. b	4. b	4. c	4. a	4. c	4. b
5. d	5. c	5. a	5. c	5. b	5. c
6. a	6. d	6. b	6. a	6. c	6. a
7. b	7. b	7. c	7. b	7. a	7. b
8. a	8. c	8. d	8. c	8. b	8. c
9. c	9. b	9. a	9. a	9. c	9. c
10. b	10. c	10. b	10. c	10. a	10. a

Final Answer Key

1. a	11. c	21. b
2. b	12. b	22. a
3. c	13. c	23. b
4. b	14. a	24. c
5. a	15. b	25. d
6. b	16. c	26. b
7. c	17. b	27. a
8. c	18. a	28. b
9. a	19. d	29. a
10. b	20. a	30. b

Optional Games

Drawing Game

To play the drawing game you will need to write or type different events from the book you are studying. Such as if you are studying the book of John one of the events could be "Jesus praying for the disciples." After you have all the events you want depicted write or typed, print them out, then cut out each individual event so there is one event on a slip of paper.

Fold each slip of paper and place it into a zip-loc bag or a bowl.

Divide your class into two teams.

Have a child from Team 1 come up to the front of the class and draw a slip of paper out of the bag. After he or she has picked an event, he or she will draw a sketch to depict that event on the whiteboard. Both teams watch as the child draws the event. When a child from either team thinks they know what is being drawn they may raise their hand and you will call on the child whose hand you see first to give their answer. It can be a child from either team. If the answer is not guessed correctly continue to call on different kids until someone guesses the correct answer.

The child who guesses the event receives 100 point for their team. Then, the teacher asks that child a question that goes with that event. For example, if the event was Daniel's being cast into the lions' den, the teacher might ask, "WHO was thrown into the lions' den?" If the student answers the question correctly he or she receives another 100 points for their team for a total of 200 points. If the child answer incorrectly, a child from the other team gets a chance to answer the question and receive 100 points for their team, with each team receiving 100 points.

After the point are given, it's Team 2's turn to pick an event out of the bag and draw it. Go back and forth with each team until each event is picked and drawn on the whiteboard, asking questions after each event is drawn.

You may want to reward the winning team with a treat like a small piece of candy or a privilege.

The Matching Game

You need at least ten questions and answers from the lesson you are studying.

Type the answers on a sheet of paper. Make two sets of answers and cut the answers into individual strips and place each set of answers in an envelope.

Divide your class into two teams. Pick a student from each team and have them come up and stand in front of you, opposite each other (back to back) in the middle of the room. On each side of the room you have taken the answers out of each envelope and mixed them up and placed them in two piles on the floor.

You ask a question and tap the two students in front of you and say "Go." They have to run from you to their side of the room and look for the correct answer to the question you just asked in their pile. If they bring you an incorrect answer, tell them, "Wrong, try again" and they race back again to find the correct answer. The first one to race back to you and bring you the correct answer gets 100 points for their team. You continue to do this until you have answered all your questions and the team with the most points wins.

Optional Games

M&M® Draw

If you are working with one student you can still play the game by asking the questions and letting the child answer and draw an M&M® if he/she answers correctly. Tell them if they get to a certain number of points they will receive a reward or privilege.

You will need a bag of M&Ms®. Empty them into a container you can't see through. Write the point values for the M&Ms® on a white board for all the kids to see. I choose point values depending on how many there are of each color—the more there are of a color the lower the point value.

Brown: 100 points

Red: 200 points

Yellow: 300 points

Green: 400 points

Blue: 500 points

Orange: 600 points

Divide the kids into two teams and ask a question from the lesson or book you are studying. If the kid you pick from the first team answers the question correctly, he or she closes their eyes and picks an M&M® from the container. Once they have chosen a color, they get to eat the candy and you record the points they won on the board for their team. If they miss the question, the other team gets to steal the question and draw the M&M®; then it's that team's turn to answer a question. The team with the most points wins.

Reward them with a small piece of candy or a privilege.

Optional Activity

Statue Maker

A fun idea to help kids is to allow one of the kids to be the statue. Use fabric and wrap his or her head in gold, their breast and arms in silver fabric, their belly and thighs in bronze fabric. You can use a pair of black sweatpants for the legs of iron to show a divided kingdom. Use black socks and sew black men's work gloves to the socks and stuff the fingers. Use a copper colored craft paint on the fingers of the gloves to represent the partly clay. Take a ball and let it hit the child's feet as the child crumbles to the ground.

Later on as you see Nebuchadnezzar on the scene, you can remind the kids with the gold fabric, he is the head of gold, and use the other fabrics for each of the other kingdoms. Use the ball to remind them of the stone that becomes a great mountain and fills the earth.

Learn how

you can be involved in "Establishing People in God's Word" at **precept.org/connect**

 Precept.org/connect

Use your smartphone to get connected to Precept's ministry initiatives! **Precept.org/connect**

Precept Online Community

provides support, training opportunities, and exclusive resources to help Bible study leaders and students.

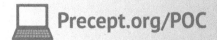 Precept.org/POC

Use your smartphone to connect to Precept Online Community! **Precept.org/POC**

 *Join The Discover 4 Yourself Inductive Bible Studies for Kids! Group in Precept Online Community*

CPSIA information can be obtained
at www.ICGtesting.com
Printed in the USA
BVOW07s0804270218
508732BV00006B/17/P